KEEPIN' THE PEACE

EARLY-DAY JUSTICE ON COLORADO'S WESTERN SLOPE

BY JUDY BUFFINGTON SAMMONS

WESTERN REFLECTIONS PUBLISHING COMPANY®

Lake City, CO

ISBN 978-1-932738-75-9

Cover and text design: Laurie Goralka Design

First Edition
Printed in the United States of America

Western Reflections Publishing Company®
P.O. Box 1149
951 N. Highway 149
Lake City, CO 81235
www.westernreflectionspublishing.com

For my grandchildren
Greg and Kayla

Table of Contents

Introduction

They all had a certain "look" the early day marshals and sheriffs of Colorado's Western Slope. They may have differed in age or physical appearance, but in many ways they closely resembled each other. Old photographs show them, one and all, looking resolute, steely eyed, deadly serious . . . dangerous. They didn't smile for their pictures but usually dressed well (for the times), often wearing some kind of suit coat, a watch chain, possibly a bandana around the neck, or even a bow tie. The badge, be it star shaped, round, or octagon, was prominent on the left breast. A handlebar moustache often completed the picture, topped by anything from a derby to a sombrero, to the wide-brimmed hat of the cowboy. Ramrod straight and often sporting a Colt holstered at the hip, they look out from old photographs with a steady gaze, reminding one that Western Colorado's raw new effort to become civilized had better be taken seriously.

As state and town governments organized in Western Colorado in the late 1870s and early 1880s, the first order of business was usually to appoint law enforcement officials. A chief of police (or marshal) and his policemen enforced laws at the local level. The counties elected sheriffs who depended on deputy sheriffs and posses to fill in with man power when things were too much for one man to handle. Sometimes a local lawman would hold a dual title, that of sheriff *and* U.S. Deputy Marshal, thus increasing his range of authority. The U.S. Marshal, of course, topped the pyramid of law enforcement tiers.

The outlaws who roamed Colorado's Western Slope were perhaps a little more loosely organized than their counterparts, the lawmen, and generally not nearly as distinguished looking. Often the only photograph that remains of one of the outlaws was that taken by a photographer after the desperado, in a failed bank robbing attempt, was gunned down. He is shown propped up against a wall, minus his shirt so that the many bullet holes in his torso can be viewed. At this point he looks dirty and unkempt—sports a farmer's tan, rumpled hair, and glazed over eyes. He looks, well . . . dead.

The subjects of these descriptive portraits, both the outlaws and the peace officers, have always drawn interest. Perhaps it is because of the way early-day law enforcement developed—arising, as it did, out of raw necessity—its start shaky and unorganized and dogged by error. After the departure of the Native Americans, the wide open West—of which Western Colorado was a prominent part—cried out for some kind of law and order as the homesteaders, gold and silver miners, weary Civil War veterans, fortune seekers, and fugitives from justice began to fill in its vast acreage.

There were few people on the Western Slope at this time. It was very rural except for mining and railroad towns. It was an immense place—thousands of square miles comprised of great quiet valleys, craggy mountain ranges, sagebrush flats, open parks, sparkling blue lakes, and rushing streams—all just there for the taking. And the "taking" of it (in a lawful way) was what most newcomers had in mind; but there were also a number of those who were bent on "taking" it any way they could. Early day desperadoes brazenly jumped claims, rustled cattle, stole horses, held up stage coaches and trains, and sometimes shot up the town just for the hell of it. Predatory men of all kinds began to fill up this new country right alongside their more law abiding neighbors.

It was a tough situation—all this wide open space—and all the various kinds of ambition that went along with it. It took quite a lot of effort to bring it all under some kind of control. In the early years, criminals were sometimes caught before jails were built to house them. Men (and women) were often hung before they had a chance at a fair trial. Once a legal system was established, trials were held at a variety of locations that were available, even saloons before court houses were built.

Keepin' the Peace takes a look at these early days of law enforcement in Western Colorado—the brazen criminals, the intrepid lawmen, the inhuman jails, and the merciless vigilante "neck tie parties." Every town had its share of incidents involving crime and justice, and it was almost always recorded in the early-day newspapers, although not always correctly. In towns stretching from Western Colorado's southern New Mexico border north to Wyoming—from Creede to Gunnison, to Delta and on up to Brown's Park and at every other new settlement in between dangerous and exciting events took place on a regular basis.

There are widely divergent renditions of some of the stories featured in *Keepin' the Peace*, especially those about bank and train robberies. The versions in the following vignettes are not the final say, but are representative of the historical research performed.

CHAPTER 1

Wide Open

*"Those who live by the gun, usually die by the gun,
be he peace officer or outlaw."*
Early-day western Colorado Sheriff, "Doc" Shores.

*"Judge John Gray has taken part in the trials of
some twenty-five especially noted murder cases . .
. he tells how they tried two men for murder 'after
supper' in Lake City one night."*
Memoirs of Judge John Gray of Montrose 1841-1940

"God did not make all men equal, Colonel Colt did."
Well known saying in the Old West

*"I have ridden across the desert between Delta and
Grand Junction when one's hand went to his gun
when a stranger was sighted."*
Millard F. Tillery, Sheriff of Montrose County in the late 1800s

B eautiful Western Colorado had been home
to the Ute Indians for over 500 years by the

late 1870s, but from that point on it would be anything but peaceful. Almost as soon as new settlers
arrived, they began encroaching on the Native
American's sacred mountains and valleys. Finally,
having had enough, the Utes rebelled—the result
being the "Meeker Massacre," quickly followed by
the inevitable "treaty"—another word for treachery,
perhaps. The treaty of March 6, 1880, resulted in the
U.S. Army's removal to northwest Utah of the Utes
from all but a small area of southwest Colorado.
The Western Slope was now open for settlement.

Newcomers began to pour into this land. Towns—
many mining boom camps—sprang up almost overnight and quickly advanced from helter-skelter villages
of tents to formally laid out streets with rough log
structures and new false-fronted buildings. Eventually
there would be churches and schools. However, all of
these new settlements, in the beginning, were a little
short of one important thing . . . law and order.

The gun that nearly every man wore on his hip
or the rifle that he carried in his saddle scabbard
tended to pass for what little there was of jurispru-
dence. Thousands of frontiersmen had seen service
in the Civil War and had come west with the standard
weapons of that conflict—revolvers such as the 1860
Colt .44 or something similar. Later, many men were
armed with some version of Colt's Peacemaker .45.
There was no shortage of armed men in the frontier
towns when the "law of the gun" initially was the only
law around.

Unfortunately if there was no shortage of guns
in the newly established towns, there was also no
shortage of liquor. Every new hamlet was graced
with numerous saloons, and they were as rough as

the "tent towns" that they catered to in the beginning. A wagon containing oak barrels of whiskey would pass for a saloon in a pinch and so would a tent. Soon, with drinking a most common pastime, a proper saloon would be constructed . . . usually more than one. When finished, a new drinking establishment would usually sport a long bar that ran along the length of a wall and was made out of dark wood. The fancier bars were backed with diamond dust mirrors. Puncheon floors and swinging doors were common, as was the standard art work that graced many saloons. A large portrait often hung over the bar portraying a nude or scantily dressed woman of generous proportions—one who possibly provided an opportunity for "wishful thinking" by men living in towns where females were initially very scarce. Games of faro and stud poker provided entertainment and so did the inevitable fights—some violent enough to end with a killing.

There seemed to be a different mindset in that day and age. There were many more poor people, fewer jobs, and life was not held as dear. Most men in mining camps were working seven days a week for months at a time. They liked to raise a little hell when they did finally find some time off, and so did the cowboys.

In every newly incorporated town, a county sheriff or a town marshal was appointed as quickly as possible. They were needed to deal with the lawlessness that went alongside the rough conditions, plentiful whiskey, and restless men wearing firearms. Who were these early-day law enforcers? In many cases just about anyone who could shoot straight and was undaunted by the prospect of tracking down dangerous fugitives who had vanished into the nearby mountains and valleys. The job also required someone who had the audacity to face down brazen outlaws on the streets of town, risking his life, and getting little in the way of compensation in return. Some of the newly appointed law men were already pretty good at this sort of thing—in fact, they had reputations that preceded them as expert gunmen . . . even former "hired guns." Some, of course, were of a different breed—just upright men, in the eyes of their contemporaries, who might be able to handle the job. Often they had no formal training. The early-day sheriffs and marshals needed help from time to time and had to depend on deputies that were usually appointed from their ranks for assistance. Some of these were trustworthy and some inept. Posses were appointed when the need arose, their job usually being to track down bank robbers or cattle thieves. When things got difficult, it wasn't unheard of for some of the less courageous posse members to give up the chase and return to town.

When compared with today's peace officer, the West's early-day sheriffs and marshals worked at a distinct disadvantage on several levels. Descriptions of "wanted men" might be ambiguous. Wanted posters were mailed out but a lot of wrong information was passed on in them. Methods of communication were dismal or non-existent—the telegraph existed in some places, but for a long time there were no telephones. There was no system in place for fingerprinting, no tracking dogs, no psychological profilers, no fast cars with sirens, and often no one to back-up the officer. There was only a dogged brave man outfitted with a tin star, a horse, and a gun.

Outlaws on the run enjoyed the advantage in the West's vast provinces and frequently were able to escape into a remote area after committing a crime. However, those who committed the lesser offenses of vagrancy, discharging firearms, or selling liquor without a license could be rounded up, tried, fined, or briefly put in jail. Those who committed more serious crimes, such as armed robbery, horse and cattle theft, rape, or murder, would usually have to be hunted down. Some of these men on the run, while at heart cowards, were also as cold blooded and murderous as they come—desperate enough to shoot a pursuing lawman from ambush. Before the West was tamed, many a good lawman met his fate this way.

Those criminals who were caught, tried, and sentenced, sometimes never had a chance to see the inside of a jail before a local lynch mob took the law into its own hands and hanged the prisoner from the nearest tree branch. If a desperado did find himself in jail, he was usually better off than his counterpart who had been hanged, but it was not a comfortable place to be. Early jails were cold in winter, hot in summer, often having only bars in the windows and no glass. Frequently, early jails were only a one-room shack, not impossible to escape from, or they were something more substantial resembling an iron cage. Bug infested, often filthy, overcrowded, and housing disreputable company, an incarcerated outlaw might even begin to consider changing his ways.

The judicial system was as untried in the West at this time as were all the other facets of enforcing the law. Geography played a major part in the problem. Huge districts were served by circuit riding judges, who traveled from town to town to mete out justice.

Of course, back then there were not as many laws on the books or as much paperwork as there is now, and legal procedures were much less formal. Even so, the overloaded schedules of district judges, who might travel hundreds of miles in a week, presented problems of another kind. The system these judges worked under was quite tenuous, and sometimes judges were not held in very high regard. Brawls often broke out in their courts, which before a proper court house was built in a community could be held in any building from a church to a saloon.

Colorado's Western Slope, at the turn of the century, saw more than its share of potentially lethal contests between the lawmen and the lawless. Outlaws, after finishing their "work," often holed up in that great outlaw hiding place in Colorado's northwest corner known as Brown's Park or in the rugged country of Johnson County, Wyoming, where the Hole in the Wall hideout was located. Both of these places were to see the likes of Butch Cassidy and many other famous fugitives.

Numerous other mining and railroad towns saw the drama unfold, too. In Creede, the presence of famed gunfighter Bat Masterson was enough to keep some semblance of law and order in that infamous, rip-roaring mining camp, even though Bat was only there to manage a gambling establishment. In nearby Lake City, a day's ride away, Sheriff Campbell was gunned down and justice was quickly served at the hands of the local citizens. The murderers were promptly hung. A sheriff wasn't on hand when the McCarty gang held up Delta's Farmers & Merchants Bank in 1893, but two of the McCartys met their fate anyway that day. They were shot down by the deadly aim of a local businessman, but not before they had killed an innocent bank employee—the father of several young children. The infamous Butch Cassidy made off with thousands of dollars after successfully robbing Telluride's San Miguel Valley Bank. Legend has it that the town's constable later shared in the loot.

While the more well-known and flamboyant crimes, criminals, and lawmen have been written about many times before, there are also a great number of lesser known, but equally interesting, situations to examine when one begins to look into the history of the Western Slope's individual towns. Nearly every crime committed was recorded in the local newspaper during those early days. *Keepin' the Peace* takes a random look at some well-known and some obscure crimes, and the attempts of lawmen or the local citizens to control everyday lawlessness. Delving into the cases that seemed most intriguing resulted in several short vignettes describing various towns' efforts to enforce the law. The time period on Colorado's Western Slope from the late 1800s to approximately 1930 bred enough excitement to fill several volumes. This book features but a few of those stories, providing an overall view of what it took to tame this slice of the lawless West.

CHAPTER 2

The Reluctant Vigilantes of Irwin

DESERTION PREVALENT

igh up in the Elk Mountain Range in west-central Colorado, the little mining camp of Irwin was born, flourished for a few years, and then quietly died. In the interim, between the years of 1879 and 1884, the citizens of the camp (sometimes called Ruby-Irwin) attempted to become civilized but had their share of lawlessness, as they went about the business of producing hundreds of thousands of dollars worth of silver. Irwin was located in a beautiful place, situated at 10,000 feet and set in a rose colored sub-range of the Elk Mountains aptly named the "Ruby Range." Irwin's breathtaking scenery was complimented by a nearby, sapphire-blue lake and towering mountain peaks in all directions. Thousands of silver seekers streamed into this paradise in 1879, ignoring as best they could the savage winters with bitter cold, deep snows, and deadly avalanches, and relishing the short heavenly summers amidst wild flowers, tall pines, and streams teaming with trout.

All rough-and-ready, early-day mining camps had pressing needs for some kind of law and order almost from the day they were founded. Not a year had gone by when city ordinances were enacted in Irwin in an attempt to provide the town with some sort of public security. These ordinances were quite similar to those established in many other frontier towns, written to discourage such crimes as public nudity, drunkenness, and disorderly conduct. Digging holes in Irwin's streets and alleys was also forbidden, although it is uncertain what a miner would have done if he struck

Irwin from the Forest Queen Mine.
State Historical Society of Colorado collection.

ore there. Law breakers could be fined and jailed, and Irwin *did* have a jail. With the many new saloons thriving in Irwin—providing merriment far into the night—there was occasional trouble. At least one killing took place over a card game.

While the city ordinances were written to try to keep citizens safe in the town, law and order was in short supply out in the hills, especially where claim jumping was concerned. Local miners felt they had to take matters into their own hands, as the camp began to grow and "rougher elements" began to appear. The miners sometimes found it necessary to form a "vigilance committee," organized to assist town authorities, as well as protect the prospectors who had located mining claims in the outlying districts. Irwin's vigilantes were initially a very large group— and a fearless one that swaggered, swore to oaths, and fueled each other up to perform acts of bravery. However on at least two occasions, most of the men in the vigilante group seemed to lose their nerve, becoming, in fact, very "reluctant vigilantes."

Their first attempt to "serve and protect" came about as the result of an Indian scare. In September of Irwin's first year (1879), the White River Utes revolted against agency agent, Nathan Meeker, which resulted in his death and that of eleven others at the agency. The citizens of Irwin lived in fear that the fired-up Utes might travel from their hunting camps on the North Fork of the Gunnison or from the Colorado River, up Ruby-Anthracite Creek to Irwin for a surprise attack. A log cabin surrounded by a log stockade was built and sentries posted outside; but of the 500 or so men who should have been available to guard the town, about 400 had already left for safer ground. Early Irwinte, Harry Cornwall, recalled in his memoirs many years later, "The majority of the men at Ruby (camp) were as cowardly as rats and ran like rats when the news of the outbreak reached us." The Utes finally arrived, though it was only an innocuous party of squaws, old men, and children who were making their traditional yearly trip up Ohio Pass to where it meets Kebler Pass, which was quite near the town of Irwin. When the alarm was sounded that Utes had been spotted, Irwin's brave vigilantes promptly deserted the stockade, most of the men disappearing into the woods to hide in the mines.

Cornwall also recalled that at a later date the vigilance committee was again called upon, this time to confront a group of claim jumpers. This time the vigilantes numbered around 150. The group advanced to the claim in question by the light of the moon to confront ten claim jumpers who were waiting for them and "loaded for bear." The approaching vigilante group passed through a thick timber stand on their way to the mining claim, but when they emerged from the trees, only a few of the vigilantes were still present—perhaps a dozen. Probably the deserters thought it would not be noticed if they quietly slipped away and did not appear for the showdown. The twelve brave men kept pressing on, however, until they discovered that the minter whose claim they were protecting was no longer present either. Someone said he was a Quaker whose religion did not permit fighting. After some discussion, it was decided that the remaining members of the vigilance committee were not willing to risk their lives for one who would not fight for himself. The "reluctant vigilantes" stalked back to town, according to Cornwall's memoirs, never to see action again.

In 1880, ex-president Ulysses S. Grant made a sight-seeing trip to Irwin, and most of the town's residents excitedly prepared for his visit. It turned out that Grant may well have *needed* a vigilance committee, or at least a decent security service, as an assassination plot had been hatched before his arrival. The camp's Southerners, many of whom had little or no use for the famous Civil War general, had seen an opportunity to even up some old scores. A plot was hatched to shoot Grant upon his entry to town, as soon as he stopped to speak to the crowds. Word leaked out, however, and the town's mayor cancelled Grant's speech. The old war hero rode into town in a buckboard without incident—his would-be assassins apparently losing either their opportunity or their nerve.

CHAPTER 3

Good Cop . . . Bad Cop

SHERIFF CYRUS "DOC" SHORES
AND STOCK DETECTIVE TOM HORN

Both Doc Shores and Tom Horn were law
enforcement officers in the frontier era of
Colorado's Western Slope. Shores, upon his death
at the age of ninety, had become a celebrated peace
officer, who would be recalled thenceforth as " . .
. just, fearless, and above reproach." Horn, on the
other hand, abused his power, besmirched his reputation, and died at the age of forty-three, swinging at
the end of a rope. Unlikely as it later seemed, these
two men once worked together as a team and were
very successful in the apprehension of horse thieves
and train robbers.

In the late 1890s, Doc Shores, in his capacity
as Sheriff of Gunnison County, Colorado, Deputy
U.S. Marshal, and part-time Pinkerton agent, was

trailing horse thieves from Western Colorado down
into Arizona. Upon his arrival in Arizona, he swore in
ranch foreman Tom Horn as a deputy to assist him. In
his memoirs, Doc described Tom Horn as he appeared
at their first meeting, as "a tall, dark-complected man
with a black mustache . . . an imposing figure of a

Sheriff Doc Shores in his later years.
Photo courtesy of the Museum of Western Colorado.

man—deep chested, lean loined, and arrow straight
. . . (he) had black, shifty eyes." Putting aside the
untrustworthy eyes and a further feeling that Horn
was "not the type of man one liked to argue with,"
Doc was apparently impressed enough with Horn's
horse-thief tracking skills to recommend his deputy for a job with the Pinkerton National Detective
Agency, which had a branch office in Denver. Horn
was soon employed by Pinkerton and would meet
with Sheriff Shores again in the line of duty when,
after a 300-mile chase, the two closed in on a party
of train robbers. This event would be the end of any
kind of working partnership between the two, as
Shores soon thereafter formed the opinion, which he
expressed later in his life, that Horn appeared to be
a man of no conscience. Shores stated in his memoirs that at the time of their last job together, chasing
down the train robbers, "Tom was more and more
showing a side of his character that I had never seen
before . . . moody, insisted on his own way . . . I made
a point of never working with him again."

These two lawmen, however brief their association in the line of duty, were the epitome of the labels
"good cop—bad cop," each earning a reputation that
bore this early assessment out. Doc Shores started
out his career in law enforcement in 1884 as a small
town sheriff employed in the rough frontier town of
Gunnison, Colorado. Already hardened by his adventures in the West when he reached Gunnison, he was
a tall, thin, but powerfully built man, looking every
inch the part of a frontier lawman. He was said to
have "kindly, but piercing eyes" and was judged to be
a man who could "think on his feet." He served eight
years in the capacity of sheriff of Gunnison County,

his reputation becoming sterling along the way.
Eventually he moved on to Grand Junction, Denver,
and Salt Lake City, serving as a railroad detective
and in other law enforcement roles. Al Look, author
of *Unforgettable Characters of Western Colorado*,
aptly described Doc Shores: "His method of catching criminals was tedious, without fanfare, without
bugles sounding a charge. He had no radio on his
saddle, used no wire tapping device, and there were
very few telephones when Doc accepted the keys to
the Gunnison, Colorado jail." Look goes on to say,
"Doc went his quiet way without the blustery blood
and thunder usually attributed to the early day law
man . . . he never killed a man. No one ever had nerve
enough to call his draw . . . he was absolutely fearless
and went after criminals to the end of the trail . . . ."

Tom Horn took an entirely different track.
While Shores had indeed recommended Horn to
the Pinkerton Agency in good faith, and while Tom
seemed to have worked successfully there for two
years, Shores' trust in him further evaporated when
Tom changed jobs. In 1892, Horn went to work as
a stock detective for John Clay, president of the
Wyoming Stock Growers Association and manager
of the huge Swan Land and Cattle Company. Horn's
job was to apprehend cattle rustlers. From that time
on, Tom Horn was little more than a hired killer. Doc
Shores again recorded his low opinion of Horn in his
memoirs, stating that, "His real fame and immortality
in cowboy legends was to come later when in 1892 as
a 'stock detective' he began to kill cattle rustlers and
sheepmen for the cow barons in Utah, Colorado, and
Wyoming. . . Horn stood out from all the rest because
of the small value he placed on human life . . . he

became a professional killer, or 'cattle rustler exterminator,' as he called himself, shooting victims from ambush for his customary price of $600 per head."

Doc Shores' assessment of Tom Horn, formed years before Tom's demise, proved to be an accurate one. After a decade of acting as a hired gun, Horn made a fatal slip, ambushing and killing a fourteen year old boy. Controversy continues to this day concerning his guilt or innocence, but nevertheless he was hung for the crime. This intelligent and fine-looking man—expert in both the fast draw and the ambush, but also cowardly beyond question—went to the gallows bravely. It is recorded that he was, in fact, the coolest man present on the occasion of his execution, expressing no guilt for his past, about which he

Tom Horn in jail, shortly before his execution.
Photo courtesy of Wyoming State Archives,
Department of State Parks and Cultural Resources.

had stated earlier, "Killing men is my specialty. I look upon it as a business proposition, and I think I have a corner on the market." A modern-day police profiler would probably label Horn a psychopath. After the execution, his body was transported from Wyoming to Boulder, Colorado, where a brother resided. He is buried in a cemetery there, his grave marked by a stone that simply states: "In Loving Memory of Tom Horn 1861-1903." Many historians have recorded his ill-fated life, making the one time lawman, if not a hero, at least an infamous figure in the history of the West's desperadoes.

Doc Shores lived a long life, earning the esteem of all who knew him, as well as the guarded respect of the train robbers, cattle thieves, and bank robbers he relentlessly pursued all his life. He was an old man when he died, but he still retained the hard muscled, eagle-eyed look he had possessed as a young lawman. He was still able to keep up a brisk pace, and, fortunately for posterity, was effective in recording his great store of memories as a lawman. Shores died in 1934 and is buried near Gunnison the town that gave him his start in law enforcement and where, from the beginning, he was as "good a cop" as Tom Horn was "bad."

(We'll hear more of Doc Shores later in this book. Doc Shore's original diary is available at the Colorado Historical Society. It was edited by Wilson Rockwell and published in the form of a book titled *Memoirs of a Lawman*.)

CHAPTER 4

Gunnison Hosts the Gunfighters

🌿 WYATT EARP AND DOC HOLLIDAY 🌿

Most people don't realize just how much time Wyatt Earp and Doc Holliday, the famous gun fighters, spent in Colorado. When hearing those well-known names, they usually think of Arizona and New Mexico. But the two men did spend a considerable time in Colorado and especially on the Western Slope. Earp and Holliday arrived in the fledgling town of Gunnison in 1882, not long after the famed "gunfight at the O.K. Corral." Gunnison was booming at this time and they found a pretty lively place. Accounts vary as to when they each arrived and how long they stayed, but Gunnison's old-timers claimed that indeed the town briefly hosted two of the West's most famous gunfighters.

Upon reaching Gunnison, Wyatt Earp and a few of his companions camped on the outskirts of town about two miles west along the Gunnison River. Doc Holliday may have been part of this group or he may have arrived later. The local newspapers noted the Earp party's arrival, stating that they looked prosperous, appeared well-armed, and owned a good camp outfit and a handsome team of mules.

Gunnison was a typical boom town at this time—rough and primitive, but beginning to show some of the signs of the arrival of civilization. Newspapers had been established and a crude water supply coursed through ditches that had been dug down either side of a wide main street. The county courthouse was under construction, and there were numerous boarding houses, restaurants, and log buildings, as well as many residential tents. A bank had been opened, a killing or two had taken place, and more than one sermon had been preached. However, while plans were underway for building schools and churches, saloons and gambling houses were being built much faster. Among the town's citizens were numerous card sharks and dance hall girls. Special red light districts thrived in the new town and, according to some historians, so did more than a dozen saloons. Many of these establishments were open all night long, and the liquor flowed freely while gold pieces changed hands across tables. It was as good a place as any for a gunfighter.

By the time Wyatt Earp and Doc Holliday arrived in Gunnison, they had each earned their membership in a very select group—they were both among the top ten gunfighters in the West. Living legends—their reputations preceded them. Many of the celebrated

Gunnison, Colorado in the early 1880s, about the time that Doc Holliday and Wyatt Earp walked its streets.
Photo courtesy of the Gunnison Pioneer Museum,
Walt Barron photographer.

gunmen of that day had at one time or another served as peace officers, often combining this occupation with the more lucrative one of gambler. Wyatt and Doc had served in these dual roles and, in so doing, both had honed to a fine edge the skill of the quick draw. Quite proficient in executing their duty as a lawman or a killer, each could perform their job with a steady hand and a cool demeanor. It was said that either of them could remove their Colt .45 from its holster and in a split second lay an opponent out dead on the floor.

The Earp party, camping by the Gunnison River, reportedly remained to themselves initially, only rarely going into town for supplies. It was rumored

they were "lying low" until some of the Tombstone
"trouble" had blown over. Eventually though, Wyatt
relocated to Gunnison, where he operated a gambling house and saloon, running a faro game in a
ramshackle two-story building on the second block
of Main Street. He was a remarkably good looking
man—tall, dark moustached, blue-eyed, and imposing, with a gun holstered high up under each arm.
While in Gunnison he likely dressed as other gun-
fighter/gamblers of the time did, wearing a distinc-
tive black broadcloth suit and immaculate white
shirt with a black string tie. An early-day newspa-
perman from the *Gunnison Daily News-Democrat*
interviewed Wyatt and reported that while he talked
freely enough, he was very cautious about what he
said. Wyatt stayed in Gunnison for a year or so, with
no particular trouble arising, everyone keeping in
mind Wyatt's stated philosophy of gun fighting ". . .
stay calm, keep your mouth shut and take your time .
. . don't 'figger to pull the trigger but once." According
to the newspapers, Earp had offered his services to
the local sheriff should the need arise. Apparently it
never did.

When Wyatt's friend, Dr. John H. (Doc) Holliday,
arrived in town, he also came with a reputation. Doc,
a former dentist, was a renowned gunfighter—in
fact he was known as one of the West's deadliest. A
thin, light-haired man with cold and expressionless
light blue eyes, Doc was afraid of nothing. He was
reputed to drink heavily and had a reputation for lur-
ing unsuspecting adversaries into fights. His uncon-
trollable temper added to the danger. In general he
was not well liked; but he, nevertheless, earned the
guarded respect of colleagues and adversaries for his

willingness to risk his life for the sake of a friend or a good cause. Doc was a steadfast follower and supporter of Wyatt Earp, and Earp returned this respect. He once stated that his friend Holliday " . . . was the most skillful gambler, the nerviest, fastest, deadliest man with a six-gun I ever saw." The press noted Doc's presence in town, as they had Wyatt's. *The Gunnison Daily News-Democrat* stated that he " was dressed in a dark close fitting suit of black, and wore the latest style of round top hat. His hair was seen to be quite gray, his moustache sandy, and his eyes a piercing blue." "I'm glad to see you, Mr. Reporter," Doc said in the interview, "but I'm not traveling about the country in search of notoriety. . . ." When asked if he'd had some trouble in Tombstone, Doc replied, "You might call it trouble."

Other than the brief reports made in the local newspapers, Earp and Holliday seemed to have made little news—certainly no headlines—in the fledgling town of Gunnison. In fact, very little is known of what happened during their stay.

Wyatt Earp moved on, continuing his habit of wandering through the West's many boomtowns, investing in mines, and running gambling establishments. After he left Gunnison, he worked as a gambler in Trinidad, Silverton, Aspen, and Denver. He lived to be eighty-one years old, his gun fighting days mostly behind him by the time he left Gunnison. Doc Holliday moved on to Silverton and then Leadville, where he shot a man. He also spent time in Denver and Pueblo. He was already ill by the time he resided in Gunnison and died on May 8, 1887, in Glenwood Springs, Colorado, of what was then called "consumption" (now called tuberculosis). The famous

gunslinger was only thirty-six when disease not a bullet brought him down.

(This article was previously published in *The
Gunnison Country Magazine*, 2008)

CHAPTER 5

Creede's Adolescent Gunfighter

❦ YOUTH GETS EVEN ❦

I n the late 1800s, Creede was considered to be one of the most notorious of Colorado's early mining camps. Creede was the last of Colorado's big silver discoveries and during its boom stage was home to thousands of people, among them such notables as Calamity Jane, Bat Masterson, and the famous card shark, Poker Alice Tubbs. It is a heartbreakingly beautiful place, located near what is now the La Garita and Weminuche Wilderness Areas. Surrounded by alpine valleys through which run clear mountain streams and the Rio Grande River, Creede was for awhile one of the most productive silver mining districts in the state and also produced its share of gold, lead, and zinc.

Creede grew quickly from a rough camp to a boomtown of 10,000; and by 1892, at its zenith, its population had grown to an estimated 30,000. Rough, two-story frame buildings were being built on its streets almost overnight. Gambling houses flourished, and law and order was in short supply. Bat Masterson was in Creede at this time, running a gambling establishment. Folks in Creede respected Bat's reputation with a gun, and some thought his presence helped to prevent trouble. In time, the town became violent, and many shootings took place. Bat, by then a little older and wiser, did not take part in any of them. However, one very young and unknown "whipper-snapper" allegedly did.

Creede (formerly named Jimtown) Main Street, May, 1892.
Officer family collection, Creede Historical Society Archives.

CREEDE'S ADOLESCENT GUNFIGHTER

This young man's activities were recorded by Sam Ashley, a man who claimed to have been familiar with the early day activities of Creede, having lived nearby during the boom days. Some of his memoirs were published, along with his obituary, in the *Saguache Crescent* in February of 1939. According to Ashley, an unnamed youth in Creede once felt called upon to settle a score with a gun. Untried as he was, he still operated as skillfully as the most experienced gun fighter. Perhaps profound anger fueled his nerve and sharpened his skill on this occasion.

Little is known of the youth's background—only that he had come to Creede from the swamps of Louisiana, found a partner in an old man whom he held in high regard, and joined forces with him to work in the mines. The boy and the old man managed to save hundreds of dollars, which they stashed in the cabin where they both lived. But there were plenty of people in Creede besides prostitutes who were adept at "mining the miners," and the boy came home one night to find his partner missing. Suspicious, he went out looking for him and eventually found him in a "dive" and in the company of "tin horn gamblers and small-time gunmen." The old man was drunk, and the boy, sizing up the situation, attempted to take him home before all their hard earned money was gambled away. At this point, one of the gamblers bludgeoned the boy with the nearest thing handy—a six shooter. Dazed and covered with blood, the young man staggered from the room with the parting remark, "I am not armed, but I will be back." Still fueled by anger, he wasted no time returning, not even cleaning up the blood still dripping from the wounds that had been inflicted on his head. Then, in the glare and glitter of the bright lights of the saloon, the youth proceeded to level the playing field. With two guns blazing, he shot three men at the table, one several times. His aim was true all three died. It was reported that after the shooting the lad calmly walked through the crowded saloon shoving cartridges into his gun, departed silently through the back door, and never was heard of in Creede again.

Escaping, as he probably did, into the rugged canyons outside of Creede, the boy slipped away, leaving the townsfolk to always wonder . . . was this sickening act of violence his first and last as a gunfighter, or did he go on to join the ranks of the West's professional killers? This unfinished story, with many pieces missing, is now all but forgotten in the sleepy town of Creede where Cy Warman, editor of an early-day local newspaper once wrote:

"It's day all day in the day-time
And there is no night in Creede."

CHAPTER 6

Death in the 'Dobies'

SHERIFF LIVES TO TELL THE TALE

C attle rustling has always been considered a grave offense by the ranchers in the West. In the early days, ranchers who had cattle stolen sometimes took matters into their own hands, serving quick justice with a rope and the branch of a tree or the roof beam of a barn. But for those skilled in the tricky business of brand changing and hell-bent on cattle thieving, the possibility of getting hanged did not serve as much of a deterrent. Unwatched cattle could be taken fairly easily, and the temptation was great.

Catching the audacious thieves was where underpaid early-day sheriffs came in—most earned little in the way of salary but could earn thousands of dollars of reward money in the pursuit and arrest of horse and cattle thieves. Such an apprehension by a sheriff took place in Colorado's infamous badlands in 1882.

The 'dobies' are a barren landscape of hills and gullies found in the drainage of the Gunnison River between Delta and Grand Junction. They form a bleak landscape that once was more green and grassy until over-grazed by sheep and cattle. Author Muriel Marshall describes them in her book *Awesome 'Dobie Badlands* as a moonscape . . . "the kind of landscape big telescopes revealed on the dead surface of the moon . . . austerely beautiful as a piece of moon fallen to earth."

It was in the 'dobies' that a sheriff tangled with cattle rustlers in 1882. The results were both tragic and comic. A huge mix-up resulted, involving the over- eager press and overzealous mourners.

It was reported by a local newspaper that Gunnison's Sheriff, John Bowman, had been shot while in the pursuit of cattle rustlers. The account given was that three rustlers had shot and killed Bowman while he was in pursuit somewhere between Grand Junction and Delta. Unfortunately the newspaper was erroneous on several counts—the main one being that it was a rustler who had been killed by the sheriff and not the other way around.

Friends and relatives of Sheriff Bowman were outraged after reading of his alleged death. There was talk of revenge; but in the meantime, a party was organized to retrieve the body, and plans went into effect to have a first class funeral for the fallen peace officer. Shortly afterwards, another message was received in Gunnison—from Bowman himself—stating that he was alive and well and was sending greetings to his friends and family.

The sad funeral rites planned for the sheriff were turned into an impromptu parade and celebration held in his absence while he waited to return to Gunnison. Carriages were secured and decorated and the would-be pall bearers rode down the street in them, reportedly wearing wide smiles. Sheriff Bowman later expressed his appreciation to the community in a letter to the *Gunnison Review*, in which he stated among other things, "I feel I ought to offer some sort of apology for not being dead."

Perhaps this incident provided some light-heartedness to what were sometimes rather dull duties in the life of a sheriff. Stacks of paper work, tax collection, killing stray dogs, and keeping the jail in order could hardly compare to staving off one's own funeral, and Sheriff Bowman had a chance to see how much he was appreciated and missed after he "died."

*Sheriff John W. Bowman.
Faded picture on the wall
of the Gunnison County
Sheriff's office.*
Walt Barron photo.

CHAPTER 7

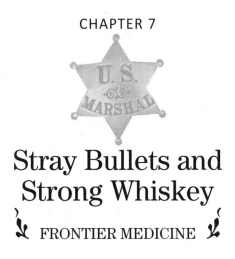

Stray Bullets and Strong Whiskey

❧ FRONTIER MEDICINE ❧

F or those men brave enough to engage in either law enforcement or law breaking around the turn of the century (be they sheriff, town marshal, gun fighter, cattle rustler, or bank robber) there was one common denominator—guns, bullets, and the resulting wounds could be very bad news.

Following the Civil War, and up to the turn of the century, America's western frontier was not the healthiest place to live; and many, including lawmen, the lawless, as well as the pioneers, did not survive its hardships for long.

Frontier doctors were few and far between, and those who were available often had little formal training. Many had earned their titles by only serving as an apprentice to an established doctor for a short time and perhaps reading a few medical books in their spare time. On the frontier, just about anyone could hang out a shingle claiming to be a doctor.

Even when the West became more settled, doctors were spread pretty thin. Many served populations that were scattered sparsely over huge geographic regions. The early-day doctor didn't wear the traditional white coat but dressed in common street attire, carrying an apron with him—not always a clean one—to protect his clothes if necessary. The tools of his trade were carried in saddle bags or the standard, old fashioned doctor's black bag.

It was a lucky peace officer or outlaw who could obtain the services of a doctor in an emergency; and if an unfortunate man needed an emergency operation,

An early-day doctor's bag displayed at the Gunnison Pioneer Museum.
Walt Barron photo.

it might well be performed on a dining room table by the light of a kerosene lantern. Family members were often enlisted as nurses. Sometimes they couldn't watch or fainted, and the doctor had to carry on without assistance. The frontier doctor's medical equipment consisted of homemade splints and bandages, a few crude medical instruments, tooth forceps, and the unreliable medicines of the time. If chloroform was not available, whiskey was often used as an anesthetic. Wounds, including bullet wounds, were usually cauterized with hot irons.

Even rougher conditions existed for a needy patient out on the range or in the hills, where an amputation might need to be performed on an unfortunate man with a bullet in him. The operation would often be done by companions who had no medical training and no better tools than a meat saw and a kitchen knife and whiskey for an anesthetic. If infection had set in, this brutal operation was sometimes necessary to save a life, or sometimes the operation itself might take the man's life.

In the late 1880s, Robert Dwyer served as sheriff of Animas City (the predecessor of Durango) in southwestern Colorado. Sheriff Dwyer was trying to control a bar fight one night when he was struck by a bullet, which lodged in his neck. He claimed that the bullet did not trouble him much, and he left it in his neck for nine months, not trusting the local doctors to remove it. Eventually he traveled to the East to doctors in Detroit, Michigan and had the bullet successfully removed by doctors with more experience. Sheriff Dwyer wore the bullet on his watch chain from that point on.

With the shortage of medical care on the frontier, home remedies often served in its stead. Many of these so-called "cures" were based on "old wives' tales," superstition, and simple ignorance. Rattlesnake bites allegedly could be cured by slashing the snake bite with a hunting knife, then soaking a bandana in whiskey and wrapping it around the bite. It didn't hurt to drink some of the whiskey to calm your nerves while waiting to see what the outcome would be—life or death. A common cowboy remedy for just about everything imaginable was sage and whiskey tea—both ingredients being readily available throughout the Old West. Home medicine chests often contained laudanum—a narcotic pain killer derived from opium. This drug may have eased different types of mental anguish, if not physical, especially if one swallowed enough. There were many patients who became addicted to laudanum, and it wasn't uncommon to hear of a death caused from an overdose.

Patent medicines or "snake oil remedies" were very common in the frontier West. One called "Never Fail" claimed to "cure nervous debility, lost manhood, and decay," among other things. Patent medicines, if the advertising were to be believed, would cure just about any affliction. In fact, the makers of most of these "snake oils" studied carefully what ailments commonly afflicted people and then made sure their advertisements laid claim to curing them all. A number of the remedies contained a good bit of alcohol, which made the patient feel better, at least for a short time. Many popular bottled syrups contained an even higher-risk ingredient—they were laced with opium.

The county coroner took over where the doctor left off in cases of violent or sudden death. He would view the body to determine the cause and manner of death. If a person had obviously died of unlawful means or the cause of death was unknown, six "good and honest men" were summoned to perform a "coroner's inquest."

The U.S. Census Office officially stated that the frontier was "closed" about the turn of the century. In the coming decades, medical services would greatly improve for those who had ventured west. Those who remember the taming of the Old West as days filled with glory, romance, and adventure, often forget what "true grit" it took just to survive in this dangerous land. And even more grit was required for

For those who had come to the "end of the trail"—the final ride could be taken in style in this 1870s hearse with a glass oval window. Gunnison Pioneer Museum.

Walt Barron photo.

the precarious lives that the lawmen and the lawless lived during this time.

(Parts of this article were previously published in *The Fence Post* — Western Slope Edition)

CHAPTER 8

All in a Day's Work

🌿 A DAY IN THE LIFE OF A SHERIFF 🌿

T he West's early-day sheriffs could count on just about anything happening before a typical day was over, and the man with the badge was expected to deal with whatever came his way. While many of his duties were dreary and monotonous, such as selling tax delinquent property at the courthouse door, rounding up stray dogs or cattle, keeping his ledgers, and doing official paperwork, sometimes the job could be very exciting. A sheriff might be called on to fight a forest fire in a pinch, hold a lynch mob at bay, even face down a hired gun. And the intrepid lawman of the Old West seldom knew in advance just when or where these events would unfold.

Let us take a random look at some interesting situations that western Colorado's sheriffs faced:

Lake City's new jail, built in 1892 and filled to capacity by 1893, served its purpose for many years. It contained four cells for men downstairs and two for women upstairs. The building in which the prisoners were housed was under the protection of Sheriff Hugh Coburn in 1946, when it burned to the ground. The unfortunate sheriff, who had his pay in his pants pocket, was evidently asleep when the fire started and had on little but his long johns. To escape the fire, he jumped from a second story window, leaving his pants behind, and then watched as the jail burned and his last month's pay went up in smoke.

Ouray's Marshal O.C. Van Houten once attempted to arrest a drunk. When he did so, the man pulled a knife on him and slit his pants leg from knee to hip. Van Houten had his gun in his hand but refused to shoot. Instead, he hit the drunk over the head with his gun, took the knife away, and escorted him to jail.

Montrose's Sheriff from 1895 to 1897, Millard F. Tillery, was a highly respected lawman, but he once found himself briefly on the other side of the law. According to local sources, a prisoner in the Montrose jail was visited on election night of 1904 by two doctors, who proceeded to perform a "surgical operation" on him. The unwilling patient had previously been accused of molesting a child. Marshal Tillery, who was now out of office, must have been in on the incident because he and the doctors were all indicted on a charge of "mayhem" for their participation in the operation, and all went to trial. The luckless prisoner was taken to the hospital. From there he was removed by an unruly mob and was never heard of again. Fortunately for Tillery, the case against him was soon dismissed for "lack of evidence." Further, a petition signed by many of Montrose's citizens was brought before the local judge, who verbally dressed down the doctors and the former sheriff. In this instance they had quite successfully, it seems, taken the law into their own hands.

Grand Junction's Undersheriff Edward Innes did not fare so well when involved with a jail prisoner. An inmate was being held for "attempting to criminally assault" an eight year old child. About five months after his incarceration, the prisoner masterminded an escape, arming himself with the only thing he found readily available—a piece of kindling wood. With it, he savagely battered Undersheriff Innes on the head and made his escape from the jail. The badly injured undersheriff died the next day as a result of his injuries. The escaped prisoner was subsequently caught, tried, found guilty, and sentenced to death by hanging. This case came to light again some ninety years later, and Edward Innes' name was finally added to a list of peace officers who have died in the line of duty, located at the Colorado Law Enforcement Memorial in Golden, Colorado.

Deputy Sheriff Benjamin Scott, an early-day law enforcement officer in Grand Junction, also died in the line of duty. According to Debbie Brockett, author of *George Crawford's Attic — Dusting Off Grand Junction Colorado's Past*, "Scott, working on a horse rustling case, was crossing the Grand (Colorado) River when his ferry overturned in 1882. Spring run-off had made the river treacherous and swimming for sure was almost impossible. Scott's body was found three days after the accident."

In February of 1898, Sheriff Neiman and other law enforcement officers and ranchers in Brown's

Park teamed up to capture four notorious murderers and cattle thieves. One of the group of outlaws was captured and hung. While the lynching was underway, the posse chased the other three outlaws and eventually captured them too. They were taken to jail to await trial. They had been there less than a month when two of them managed to overpower Sheriff Neiman, knock him out, and lock him in a cell. They next stole two horses and raced off to catch a stage to transport them out of the area. They were waiting for the stage the next morning and when it at last pulled up, they discovered to their chagrin that none other than the sheriff was on it. The pair was arrested again and sent to a supposedly escape-proof jail in Aspen. A couple of months later, they bludgeoned a jailer, overpowered an unarmed sheriff, and then made their escape for a second time.

Two incarcerated men in Gunnison's jail managed to do more damage to themselves than to any lawman. According to the *Gunnison Daily Review-Press* of December 12, 1882, "Two jail birds got into a row this afternoon. . . one, up for murder, struck another in the head with a washboard. . . coming very close to laying him out." Apparently that was the end of the trouble on that particular day.

A few years later, in 1886, Gunnison's Sheriff Doc Shores experienced plenty of excitement one day when, back to back, he escorted the notorious "man eater" Alfred Packer to the courtroom and then proceeded to confine accused murder Hugh McCabe temporarily in Packer's empty iron cell. McCabe found Packer's razor in the cell and cut his throat from ear to ear with it. Shores recalled in his memoirs, "I shuddered as I looked down at his grotesquely dangling head, which was nearly severed from his body."

Shores was to discover later that the dead Hugh McCabe had used an alias and was actually Thomas Hurley, one of the most prominent members of the infamous "Molly Maquire gang."

CHAPTER 9

Early Day Jails

 VISITING THE CALABOOSE

A s the new towns of the Western Slope grew, crime kept right up with the new construction. Crimes were sometimes committed before a jail had been built. Therefore a town, even if it consisted of little more than a few rough log structures and tents, usually put the building of a jail on the top of its list of priorities. Needless to say, all kinds and manners of jails sprung up on the dusty, muddy streets of Western Colorado's brand new towns. Often, when barely finished, they would already be filled to capacity. A newly elected sheriff needed a place to put those who were charged with such acts as drunkenness, disturbing the peace, larceny, wife beating, resisting arrest, destroying property, or worse yet, rape, murder, or stealing a horse. And, of course, there were those who needed to be held in custody for what was called "mental observation."

The sheriff was often housed near or even in the same building as the prisoners, so that he or a deputy, or one of their wives, could cook for the prisoners. The typical sheriff's office had a pot-bellied stove or a cookstove—something similar to the old standard "Majestic Range." A sheriff's office might contain a roll-top desk, a safe, pegs on the wall for gun belts and keys, and, in more up-to-date offices, a typewriter for the sheriff's abundant paperwork.

The jails themselves varied in their manner of construction. Crested Butte's jail was constructed of thick stone walls and had bars on the windows. Grand Junction's original jail was built out of squared

Sheriff's office at the Saguache County Jail.

Courtesy of the Saguache Museum. Walt Barron photo.

off logs, and Cedaredge's jail was constructed of stacked boards. These types of jails proved to be solid and secure, although not impossible to escape from. Grand Junction's first jail was located in the downtown area between Main Street and Colorado Avenue and was a small square building with one room and one tiny window. It sat by itself on a dirt street and looked quite forlorn. The jail served its purpose well though, housing some of the perpetrators of four different murders committed in the first year of that town's existence. Since court in early-day Grand Junction was held only two sessions a year in May and October, the jail was usually full of those awaiting trial.

Saguache County's jail, which can still be seen when visiting the Saguache Museum, was built in 1908

Saguache County Jail.
Courtesy of the Saguache Museum. Walt Barron photo.

and sat beside a house where the sheriff or under-sheriff lived with his family. Built of adobe, it housed the sheriff's office, both men's and women's cells, and it boasted an "escape proof maximum security cage." The original jail graffiti can still be seen on its walls. A sheriff was once locked up here and held hostage in his own jail by a family member who demanded the release of a brother. In more peaceful times, when the jail was empty or a prisoner was well known, the sheriff's children felt free to roller skate around the cells or even in those that were empty.

Cooking facilities at the Saguache County Jail. Courtesy of the Saguache Museum. Walt Barron photo.

⌒

*Interior
of the
Saguache
County Jail.*
Courtesy of
the Saguache
Museum.
Walt Barron
photo.

The city of Montrose built its first primitive jail in 1883; but in 1885, an even better one was built. It measured 24 x 28 feet and was constructed entirely of stone. Its walls were high and also went four feet into the ground. An iron ceiling completed the picture of a hopefully escape-proof jail. Iron cages housed most prisoners, and the jail also boasted a 6 x 12 foot stone cell. This somewhat depressing structure has stood the test of time and still is in use for storage in Montrose's downtown business section.

In 1907 Lewis Dolf was elected as Cedaredge's first Town Marshal. Dolf, who was apparently a skilled carpenter, found his first duty as Marshal was to build the town's jail. The jail was constructed with stacked boards—2 x 6's spiked together with the six inch side lying flat. The structure, when completed, had six-inch walls that were thought to be impenetrable without a saw or shovel. In addition, the small window was heavily barred. All in all, the jail seemed to be sturdy enough seemingly escape-proof. But perhaps Marshal Dolph had not counted on the advantages enjoyed by especially skinny prisoners. One enterprising felon, a quite slim one, took down the stovepipe, tore the jail's chimney apart brick by brick one night, and likely by standing on the stove, managed to wriggle through the very small chimney hole

The town jail, now housed at Pioneer Town Museum in Cedaredge.

Walt Barron photo.

Old jail cell sitting in the yard of the Hinsdale County Museum.

Gregory Stoneburner photo.

in the ceiling. He escaped into the night never to be seen in Cedaredge again. Lewis Dolph's jail, although not escape proof, was beautifully built and used for many years. It now graces the grounds of Cedaredge's "Pioneer Town" Museum.

From reading early-day accounts, one could safely conclude that most of the first jails were not at all pleasant places to be. The small cage-like cells were cold in the winter, sweltering in the summer, and afforded little or nothing in the way of bathing facilities. Prison food could be either tasty or appalling, depending on the cook. Prisoners were given little to do to occupy their long, idle hours. Some, like Tom Horn before his execution, braided lariats or quirts; others carved articles out of deer and elk antlers. Many wrote letters or read books. Often they whiled

*Gunnison's
Pioneer
Museum
displays the
locks and keys
used in the
town's earliest
jail.*

Walt Barron
photo.

away the time in the company of other disreputable
people. There were seldom facilities that would allow
for segregation. Cells were secured with huge locks
or padlocks that were opened with three inch long
keys. Leg irons were sometimes used to control or
contain prisoners. These were heavy, large-linked,
and made of iron.

One might conclude that, with the dire conditions
existing in the original Western Slope jails, crime in
the old West would have been minimal; but the oppo-
site was unfortunately true and most of the old-time
jails were, if nothing else, very well used.

In the *Lake City Silver World* on August 26,
1876, it was reported that a drunk lady was "lugged"
to the local jail one night. The newspaper went on to
conclude:

> *"Who she was and how she fared,
> nobody knew and nobody cared."*

CHAPTER 10

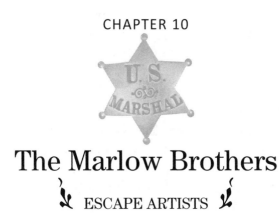

The Marlow Brothers
ESCAPE ARTISTS

T he well-known John Wayne movie, "The Sons of Katy Elder" was loosely based on the experiences of the Marlow family in Texas. The five Marlow brothers, Alfred, Boone, Charley, Lewellyn (Epp), and George lived precarious lives in the Old West. The five brothers were the sons of Martha and Williamson Marlow. The family spent most of their early years drifting around the West and "the boys" from time to time had had various scrapes with the law. Only two of them survived to an old age. Those two, Charley and George, eventually landed in Western Colorado.

In August of 1888, the five Marlow brothers were falsely accused of horse theft and arrested. By December of that year all were bonded out of jail and were awaiting trial. Boone Marlow was subsequently

accused of killing a man back in 1886. He had allegedly been cleared of that crime, but a Texas sheriff
and his deputy pursued Boone anyway and attempted
to arrest him. A gunfight resulted and the sheriff was
killed. While Boone hid out, the other four brothers
were arrested as accessories to the crime and put
back in jail. Boone was later hunted down and killed
by bounty hunters.

In January of 1889, the remaining brothers were
transported by a U.S. Deputy Marshal to a Federal
Court in Graham, Texas, to await trial, and they ended
up back in jail. A mob descended on the jail with a
lynching in mind. However, the brothers were successfully removed by peace officers late at night and
carried by wagon toward a safer town, Weatherford,
Texas. George was shackled to Lewellyn and Charley
was shackled to Alfred. En route, a mob of angry
citizens caught up with them. A battle resulted and
two of the brothers were killed. George and Charley
were wounded, but survived and escaped by cutting
off their brothers' feet at the ankles. They made their
get away by wagon and in time were acquitted of
all charges against them. Members of the mob that
had ambushed the four brothers were eventually
prosecuted.

Later, after the trouble had died down, George
and Charley made their way to Colorado. They
apparently "went straight" and tried their hand at
a ranching enterprise about two miles south of the
town Ridgway. This town is located some thirty
miles south of Montrose. It sits in the picturesque
Uncompahgre Valley and is surrounded by mountains of the Cimarron and Sneffles Ranges. The
Marlows lived in this beautiful area for many years,

both serving as Deputy U.S. Marshals. The former fugitives also found employment as deputy sheriffs in nearby Ouray. In the dual roles of law enforcement and ranching, they seemed to perform quite respectably.

In 1886, George Marlow had visited the town of Gunnison and made the acquaintance of Doc Shores, Gunnison's famed lawman. Later in 1891, when Doc needed twenty-four deputies to assist with a Crested Butte miners' strike, he called upon the Marlow brothers for assistance. They had a reputation as being tough and capable gunfighters. By telegram, Doc invited Charley and George to come by train to Gunnison to assist in dealing with the deadly strike. The brothers left immediately to go to Doc's aid. They each strapped on a .45, took up a sawed-off Winchester, boarded the train, and headed for Gunnison.

Once there, they were deputized; and, armed to the teeth, they accompanied Doc to a potentially explosive meeting in Crested Butte. Prior to this meeting, a shootout had taken place between law enforcement officers and the striking miners, and tempers were still flaring. Present at the meeting were mine officials, striking miners, Sheriff Shores, and several other deputies besides the Marlow brothers. Doc relied on the Marlows to put on a show of force and they did not disappoint him. Charley Marlow reported in his memoirs that he helped set the tone for the tension-filled meeting by jumping up on a table with a .45 in each hand and stating boldly: "Boys, I got up here so that I could see just what was going on; I can see every part of the room; I am for peace, but if any man pulls a gun, he will not live long enough to regret his rash act."

The meeting finally ended peacefully with some tentative agreements being made. No one had to use a .45 or a Winchester, and George and Charley left Gunnison with their wages in their pockets, a promise of a car load of coal from the mine officials, and Sheriff Doc Shore's gratitude.

The Marlows, in time, gained a pretty good reputation in Colorado. Perhaps the best description of their lives is the one that they wrote themselves. In their book, *The Life of the Marlows*, they described themselves as: ". . . typical frontiersmen, generous to a fault, faithful to a friend, scrupulously honest, and afraid of trouble, but when trouble was forced on them, their conduct under such circumstances was as certain as their acts were scientific."

CHAPTER 11

Outrage in Ouray

 CHILD MURDERERS LYNCHED

T here are few places more beautiful than Ouray, Colorado. The little village of Ouray sits like a jewel beneath a circle of towering mountains whose colors constantly shift and change with the angle of the sun. In the late 1890s and early 1900s, it was home to the famous Camp Bird Mine—for many years one of Colorado's top gold and silver producers; and it was also the location of one of the most gruesome lynchings ever executed in an early-day mining camp.

This event is particularly disturbing because it centered around an innocent child and her adoptive parents. Ten-year-old Mary Rose Mathews had already seen more than her share of hardship before being brought to the Western Colorado town of Dallas. This small frontier town was located near present-

day Ridgway, ten miles north of Ouray. Little Mary's
mother had died when she was younger, and her
father had subsequently found it necessary to place
his child in a Catholic orphanage—Denver's St.
Vincent's Home. These two events provided plenty
of emotional trauma for young Mary Rose, and add-
ing to it was her placement with an unknown family
in an unfamiliar place. In the summer of 1883, she
was put in the care of a man and his wife—Michael
and Margaret Cuddigan. The pair was attempting
to eke out a living by farming and ranching a small
homestead located in the rugged country near the
town of Dallas. When Mary Rose came to live with
them, the Cuddigans already had a young baby and
another was on the way. One could surmise that
Margaret Cuddigan took in the orphaned Mary Rose
to assist with the care of her child and the house-
hold chores.

Little is known of Mary Rose's stay with the
Cuddigans, although rumors were circulating that
she was being abused. No one stepped in however,
and in January of 1884, after a residence of only a few
months, it was reported that the little girl had mysteri-
ously died. Previous speculation rose to a fever pitch;
it was thought by many that Mary Rose's death may
not have been the result of sickness or an accident,
but rather had come about because of some form of
monstrous cruelty. Ouray County's coroner acted on
the rumors a few days later. Mary Rose's grave was
found and her body disinterred, taken to Ouray, and
examined by a doctor. It appeared that Mary Rose
had indeed suffered—her body showing evidence of
frozen feet and legs, frozen fingers, cuts and bruises,
as well as blows to the head with a blunt instrument,

which was the cause of her death. It also appeared that the child had been raped.

Armed with this information, Ouray County officials promptly arrested the Cuddigans. At this time Ouray had no jail and the couple was taken to Ouray and lodged in a local hotel under the guard of the sheriff, two of his deputies, and relatives of the Cuddigans. Ouray County's citizens were, of course, outraged upon hearing of the circumstances of Mary Rose's demise. A lynch mob was quickly formed, and the angry crowd stormed the hotel. They were faced down by the sheriff who was desperately trying to perform his duty. He reportedly answered the mob's demands by telling them to "go to hell." He and his deputies were quickly overpowered, however, and the Cuddigans were dragged from their beds and out into the frigid Ouray night. The terrified Margaret, seven months pregnant, was dragged along with her husband down Ouray's icy streets. At a location just north of town, the pair was lynched for a crime of such turpitude that it could only be equaled now by the death of Margaret Cuddigan's unborn child.

The remains of the Cuddigans were not allowed burial in the local cemetery, so they were buried on a ranch a few miles north of Ouray.

Mary Rose's unfortunate story does not end with her foster parent's hangings. She was reburied in Ouray's Cedar Hill Cemetery but had rested there only a couple of weeks when her body was disinterred again and shipped to a Denver undertaker. Denver's citizens had been horrified by the hanging of a pregnant woman, and Mary Rose's body was sent there to show justification. Her pitiful little remains were displayed to thousands of curious onlookers before she was finally buried in a Denver cemetery next to her natural mother.

In 1887 another attempt was made by a Ouray vigilance committee to take the law into their own hands. The results were as grizzly as were those of the Cuddigan case. Soon after a waitress was killed by a black man in Ouray, the man was arrested and jailed. Subsequently, nearly100 masked men descended on the home of a deputy sheriff and demanded the jail keys. The deputy convinced the mob that he did not have the keys. The mob then moved on to the jail and tried to break into it with a hammer. Being unsuccessful, they then attempted to burn the jail down. Efforts were later made to put the fire out, but this was not accomplished before the terrified prisoner died in his cell of suffocation from the smoke.

CHAPTER 12

Reformed Rustler of Brown's Park

ISOM DART

H e was uncommonly black, it was said . . . tall, muscular, and well proportioned. He was square-jawed and handsome with high cheekbones; he looked every inch the cowboy that he was. Honed by the requirements of the cattle range, Isom Dart was an expert with a rifle and a lariat and an accomplished horseman. He was an outlaw for a time during his younger years—a cattle rustler and horse thief. Then for a number of years he tried his best to leave his criminal life behind and "go straight" and he succeeded. For a while, anyway.

Ned Huddleston, who later changed his name to Isom Dart, was born a slave in the South in the mid-1800s. Throughout his life, he worked as a cook, cattle rustler, rodeo cowboy, horse thief, bronc rider, and legitimate rancher. He had been involved in the Civil War when he was a teenager, cooking for Confederate officers. When the Emancipation came, he took his chances and, along with many others, turned his horse towards the West. Perhaps thinking there was no better option for a black man with few skills, he then embarked on a career in crime. His first lucrative job involved stealing horses in Mexico and bringing them across the Rio Grande into Texas. After following a criminal life for a time, he attempted more legitimate occupations such as bronc busting. For a while, he excelled as a rodeo cowboy. However, before long he was rustling cattle again further north, and he became involved with the infamous Gault Gang.

The Gault outfit made a lucrative business out of following the horse and cattle herds as they were pushed along the Overland Trail and elsewhere. They would collect stray livestock from these herds, change brands, and add the cattle or horses to their own growing numbers of livestock.

Isom Dart had a very unpleasant experience while in the company of the Gault gang. One evening he and the gang were busy burying a fellow member who had been kicked to death by a horse. The gang was ambushed that night and all of them were killed except Isom. He survived by jumping into the grave and playing dead. Eventually he was able to crawl away and make his way to a nearby ranch where he stole a horse. He was spotted by the ranch owner and shot as he rode away. Later he fell off the stolen horse and passed out from the loss of blood. He was found on the trail by a friend who nursed him back to health. After this incident, Isom Dart attempted to go straight again.

He settled on Brown's Park in the extreme northwest corner of Colorado as a place to begin building up his own herd of cattle in the hope of becoming a legitimate rancher. The park, encompassing some of Wyoming to the north, Utah to the west, and the rest in Western Colorado, was a place of pure mountain beauty. Early on, the park had been home to various Native American tribes and, later, was frequented by mountain men and fur traders for their annual rendezvous. It was also a long-time location for wintering herds of cattle. By the time Isom arrived, the park was well on its way to becoming prime "cattle country" not just a winter hold-over spot for herds headed north and west, but a permanent home for cattlemen. Cattle outfits, from the huge ranches of cattle barons to the small quarter sections of sod busters, would soon inhabit Brown's Park. Unfortunately, the "park" also experienced more than its share of cattle rustlers, horse thieves, and outlaws.

All Dart needed to get his initial start was experience, a horse, six-gun, rifle, and a lariat. He quickly went to work for cattle outfits as an all-around top hand and an expert bronc rider. By the mid-1890s, Dart had built up a sizable herd of his own, branding them with his ID bar brand. He had also managed to win the affection and respect of many of his neighbors in Brown's Park. Isom Dart had finally "made it" and was well on his way to attaining success and respectability in the cattle business. But, unfortunately, it didn't last.

Possibly Isom Dart's only mistake at this stage of his life had been picking the wrong location for his ranch. The road through Brown's Park was part of the famous "Outlaw Trail," which had seen the likes of Butch Cassidy and his Wild Bunch and quite a few others of the same ilk. At the time Isom was there, it was also the battleground of big cattle outfits that were engaged in vicious fights over the open range with smaller stockmen or homesteaders.

And, while Dart may not have actually been involved in any of these fracases, he probably suffered the consequences by association. There were several local ranchers who suspected that he was cattle rustling, and in the summer of 1900 a note was posted on his door warning him to leave the area. On a crisp October morning of that same year, Dart stepped out of a cabin located on Cold Springs Mountain. He was

Isom Dart's grave on Cold Springs Mountain in Brown's Park.

Photo courtesy of the Museum of Northwest Colorado.

in the company of several companions, all leaving the cabin and heading for a corral to catch their horses. Suddenly, out of nowhere, a shot rang out, perhaps one not even intended for Isom Dart, but which fatally struck him anyway. It has always been suspected that he was gunned down by Tom Horn, hired killer of the Wyoming Stockgrowers Association. Whoever the shooter was, he quickly left the country, leaving the whole affair to continued speculation.

And so Isom Dart's career, both as an outlaw and a respectable citizen, was abruptly ended at the age of fifty-one. He was buried in an isolated grave on Cold Springs Mountain near his old cabin. The grave can still be seen today, surrounded by a crude wooden fence and shaded by aspen that have grown to large trees since his burial. A simple sign on the fence that surrounds the grave reads, "Isom Dart 1849-1900." Here he lies alone, overlooking the silver-green sage-brush, the summer hills radiant with wild flowers, and the winter prairie dusted with snow. Below his resting place lies Brown's Park a refuge that betrayed him.

(Parts of this article were previously published in *The Fence Post* — Western Slope Edition)

CHAPTER 13

Killing Over Water

❦ LAKE CITY AND OLATHE INCIDENTS ❦

W ater is the lifeblood of the West and the life-blood of the ranching industry. The filing of the first water rights in Western Colorado marked the beginning of a process of ownership of a commodity that was separate from but as valuable as the land itself. The area's semi-arid climate required the pioneers to find a way to provide supplemental moisture. If ranchers were to encourage the growth of native hay and other crops, irrigation water would be a necessity. The water in rivers, fed in the summer by snow melt from high in the mountains, could be diverted into ditches dug by hand or with a horse and slip, literally bringing into creation the business of cattle ranching.

Of course, water rights—with man-made priorities as to who was entitled to the water—were often

secondary to Mother Nature's dictates. An adequate
annual snowfall in the mountains, with a slow melt-
ing period in the spring, was needed to supply contin-
uous reserves of water in the first place; and, Mother
Nature was usually generous. However, the early
homesteaders and ranchers were sometimes not so
generous with each other. Conflicts over water use
arose from time to time, with none so deadly as one
that occurred near Lake City in 1899.

Lake City sits on the northern edge the San Juan
Mountains. It has always been the only town of any
size in Hinsdale County. It began as a mining camp in
1874 when gold was found in the nearby hills. Lake
City can boast of having the first church and the first
newspaper on the Western Slope. The main river
that runs through it is the Lake Fork of the Gunnison
River, which passes through Lake San Cristobal en
route to the Gunnison River. In the lake and the river
and its tributaries there seemed to be plenty of water
. . . surely enough to go around.

The *Gunnison Tribune*, August 4, 1899 reported
the following incident:

> *Another Lake Fork killing occurred . . . on a*
> *ranch not far from the Moore place. John N.*
> *Thompson, on a Monday morning in early*
> *August, rode up to Sheriff Wiley's office in*
> *Gunnison and surrendered himself, saying*
> *he had shot and killed Sam Holroyd. The two*
> *men, owning adjoining ranches, had been*
> *disputing over land and water. Holroyd had*
> *previously asked a guard to protect him*
> *while he attended to his headgates, but had,*
> *of course, been refused. The Sunday before*

Thompson's report to the sheriff, Holroyd had gone to the ditch headgate to turn on water, first strapping a Ballard rifle to his shoulder. The next morning, Holroyd's body was found, with the top of his head blown off, across the ditch near the broken embankment. A bullet had entered the right side of his head, about an inch above the ear. His rifle, which was rusty and had not been fired for some time, was still strapped to his shoulder. Thompson told his own people what he had done, and then left for Gunnison to report the shooting. Local feeling in the valley ran high, but Thompson was acquitted of murder.

Many witnesses were questioned at the trial, and many who had heard the testimony thought Thompson should have been convicted instead of the "not guilty" verdict that finally came in; but the unspoken and unwritten law of the land, which of course included water, prevailed. The jury apparently believed that a man had a right to protect his water as he would his home or family and, if necessary, with extreme measures.

The little town of Olathe, located between Delta and Montrose, was the setting for a similar incident a few years prior to the Lake City killing. Olathe is located in Montrose County and named for Olathe, Kansas. It sits on the Uncompahgre River and is a flourishing farming community.

On California Mesa, which lies a few miles west of Olathe, neighbors Mark Powers and Charles Bear had a deadly confrontation over water. Charles Bear diverted water from Power's ditch one day without the latter's permission. He was then threatened by Powers, who was carrying a rifle. Things got heated and words were exchanged, whereby Bear refused to cease his "borrowing of water." Powers lost his temper and fired, his bullet hitting home. Bear bled to death trying to crawl away from the scene.

Powers was arrested and taken to the Montrose County jail. In no time at all, word got around of Power's frightful deed, and a huge mob of men formed in nearby Delta. They made quite a picture, pounding out of Delta, headed towards Montrose on horseback, and bent on serving vigilante justice.

Because the Montrose sheriff was not available to handle the explosive situation, District Court Judge John C. Bell was called upon to try and keep matters under control. He quickly swore in twenty deputies but ordered them to remain unarmed, knowing they would be no match for the many armed men. The mob had arrived, in the meantime, and was congregated at a hotel located across the street from the jail. Five of the newly appointed deputies approached them, trying to talk them out of the forthcoming lynching.

In the meantime, a hole had been dug in the jail wall by the deputies and a team of fast horses and a wagon waited in the alley. Powers had barely squeezed through the hole and mounted the wagon when he was spotted attempting to leave town. The driver of the wagon made a desperate run for Ft. Crawford, a military post some eight miles south of Montrose. The mob followed in hot pursuit, and did not give up until the prisoner and his wagon were safely at the fort.

Although the circumstances of the Olathe killing over water were quite similar to the one that occurred in Lake City, the outcome was drastically different for the Olathe defendant. Powers was eventually returned to Montrose, where he stood trial for the killing. He was convicted of first degree murder and sentenced to die on the gallows. His case was successfully appealed and he was granted a new trial. At the second trial his sentence was reduced to voluntary manslaughter. After eight years in the state penitentiary the elderly Powers was pardoned and released. He died shortly afterwards of old age.

Mark Twain once said, "Whiskey is for drinking; water is for fighting." He might have amended it to say, "Whiskey is for drinking; water is for killing."

CHAPTER 14

Homicide at Ohio City

YOUNG HORSE THIEF MEETS HIS FATE

I n the early days on the Western Slope, a cowboy who was wrongfully deprived of his horse or a cattleman who came up short on calves often took matters into his own hands. One such incident occurred in the little community of Ohio City, located on Quartz Creek not far from the foot of Monarch Pass.

The valley where Ohio City is located was once home to the Utes. Later miners sought the region's rich deposits of silver and gold. The little mining town mushroomed and then shrank, providing a fickle population for the valley. Some people stayed on, having found gold of another kind in the rich soil of the Quartz Creek country. This small, pretty valley soon filled up with ranchers. Things were not always peaceful among the ranchers, however. Occasionally there was trouble.

"Homicide at Ohio City" was the headline of the *Gunnison News Champion*, July 6, 1906. The newspaper article went on to announce that a local cowboy, Frank Vader, had shot and killed George Cameron, horse thief. It seemed that the outlaw, who was doing some friendly drinking in the local saloon with Vader, had excused himself and gone outside. Once there, he mounted Vader's horse and took off at a dead run with not only the horse and saddle, but a rifle and a revolver as well. The surprised victim quickly secured a gun from someone in the saloon, borrowed a horse, and followed in hot pursuit. A confrontation took place further up the road with the result being that the outlaw was shot dead through the chest by Vader's borrowed .38 Colt. The young killer then gave himself up to the custody of the Gunnison sheriff, keeping in mind the advice of an attorney to keep his mouth shut.

The law at that time prevented removal of the unfortunate felon's body until the Coroner had the sheriff summon six men to perform the duty of serving as jurors at a Coroner's Inquest. The group's conclusions (after viewing the body the next day) were that the outlaw had drawn first and the cow puncher had acted in self defense. The verdict was termed "justifiable homicide." Thus justice was served quickly to the horse thief and just as quickly for Frank Vader, who at the age of twenty-two had found it necessary to take the law into his own hands.

The dead horse thief was buried not far from where he met his fate in what is now, 100 years later, a lonely and forsaken little cemetery located near Ohio City, and overgrown with sagebrush. His grave is unmarked and lies outside the cemetery's fence. A

Ohio City cemetery where outlaw George Cameron was buried outside the fence.

Walt Barron photo.

common practice in the early days was to bury out-laws and others of low station apart from the more upstanding members of the community. And so this young man, who made the foolish youthful deci-sion to steal a friend's horse, had paid with his life. There was no second chance. Quick justice had been served.

(This article was published at an earlier date in *The Gunnison Country Times*)

CHAPTER 15

Killing: 15 Cents Apiece— Two for a Quarter

❧ TELLURIDE'S MARSHAL JIM CLARK ❧

elluride, in the late 1800s, was a quaint, beautiful little mining camp located in southwestern Colorado on the San Miguel River in the western San Juan Mountains. Telluride's mines were rich in zinc, lead, copper, silver, and gold; and it was famous for its historic mines: the Tomboy, Pandora, Smuggler-Union, Nellie, and Sheridan.

Telluride's town marshal in 1895 was Jim Clark, a large, brown eyed, and heavily moustached man. He was quite a contradiction of personality traits. On the one hand, he was known to be a fearless killer, a deadly shot, and one who had little regard for human life—even less regard for women, it was said. Yet this hard, hard man had a soft side to him. He did all kinds of favors for the elderly and was always willing to help any child who needed attention. Marshal Clark was certainly an enigma in the little town of Telluride, where he quite successfully kept the peace. However he walked a fine line between keeping the law and breaking it. And he died when he was shot down from ambush on a summer's night in the streets of Telluride.

Clark had a somewhat shady early life and had drifted into Colorado after riding with Quantrell's guerilla band during the Civil War. After the war he became an outlaw allegedly riding with the Younger and Jesse James gangs. He robbed trains and held up stages. He eventually drifted into the booming town of Leadville, Colorado, in the late 1870s. There, he worked as a miner, and it was rumored that he also had a part in a stage coach hold-up or two. He arrived in Telluride in 1887, getting a job digging a trench for a pipeline. He noted the lawlessness of the town at the time and, being thoroughly aware of the ins and outs of such things, he offered his services to the mayor as a deputy marshal. It wasn't long before tough Jim Clark had cleaned up the town and was promoted to town marshal. However, it was well-known that he continued a life of crime on the side. Word was that he was a party to several hold-ups during this time, wearing a disguise that consisted of an old hat and fake whiskers.

It is said that the town elders kept him on as marshal, even though they knew he was operating on both sides of the law. Clark was so effective in his marshal job that no one could take his place. A sort of "school-yard bully"—his good qualities appeared to outweigh his bad.

Eventually, the Telluride City Council decided that Jim Clark was too much of a liability, and they asked him to resign. He refused and was subsequently fired. Shortly afterwards he was replaced by someone thought to be as tough as he was. Clark was furious and retaliated by threatening to kill the members of the City Council who had voted to fire him. He put a price on the council members' heads and was quoted as saying, "I'm in the market to kill . . . fifteen cents apiece or two for a quarter."

Gunnison's highly respected lawman, Sheriff Doc Shores, was called in to intercede. He made a special trip to Telluride and tried to reason with Clark and talk him into leaving town. In spite of Clark's bad reputation, Shores seemed to respect him and feared that Clark was a marked man if he stayed in Telluride. According to Shores' memoirs, he even wrote a letter of recommendation for his friend so that Clark might acquire a job elsewhere. He then advised him, "I understand that you've been having a little trouble with the city fathers . . . you've sort of got the lawmen of Telluride over a barrel. They won't try to arrest you or have it out with you openly because they know you're too much for them. Their only alternative is to shoot you in the back . . . If I were in your place, I'd get out of this man's town before I got bushwhacked."

Unfortunately Clark did not heed the advice. On August 6, 1895, he decided to take a stroll down Telluride's main street late at night. As he walked into the street, a shot rang out. A gunman had fired from the top of a nearby saloon. Clark fell where he was shot and was carried to his nearby cabin where he bled to death a short time later. Many thought the City Council had hired an assassin.

Clark's funeral was large and attended by both the law abiding and the lawless. After the services he was buried in Telluride's Lone Tree Cemetery in a section with other Civil War veterans. Doc Shores apparently attended the funeral and recorded the following thoughts in his book *Memoirs of a Lawman:* "That night after Clark was buried, I went down to his cabin. Tearing up a plank in the floor, I took out his slicker, cap, and false whiskers and burned them. It was the last favor I could bestow on a loyal friend, who, like most of us, had a lot of good in him as well as a lot of bad."

CHAPTER 16

Western Colorado's Sheep and Cattle Wars

"Cattlemen and sheepmen rushed to beat each other to what was left of the grasslands and good water. A collision was inevitable, and the cattlemen's angry unwillingness to share what he considered his rightful and exclusive domain led to decades of brutality and terror on the range."

Ogden Tanner — *The Ranchers*

It is rumored, but not confirmed by either written records or formal acknowledgments, that during the late 1800s and early 1900s various cattlemen's associations around the Western Slope had "anti-sheep" sub-groups. There was usually no mention of these groups in these associations' formal minutes, but their existence was assumed by many of the local citizens.

If such groups did indeed exist, they were comprised of tightly-knit companies of men whose loyalty to each other and to the cattle industry kept their activities more or less secret for decades. Only a few hints of their alleged activities leaked out from time to time, but the true facts generally remain unknown or vaguely defined—unwritten chapters of the history of the Western Slope of Colorado.

If such "take the law into your own hands" assemblies did exist in Western Colorado, they would have been no different than the groups formed by cattlemen in many other western states. In fact, it would have been unusual if such groups had not developed. Every cattleman knew of the damage that could be done to the range when it was over-grazed by huge numbers of sheep—horror stories arrived from neighboring states even before the sheep did.

At the turn of the century there were not, as a rule, extensive numbers of sheep to be found in many areas of the Western Slope's "cattle country." (An exception would be the 'Dobies near Delta.) Usually the local cattlemen's associations had successfully discouraged anyone who migrated into "their" country with sheep, unless the sheep stayed in certain designated areas. These designated areas had usually been deemed undesirable for the grazing of cattle or were not being used by the cattlemen. There was in existence a kind of gentlemen's agreement about where sheep would and would not be kept.

A number of factors contributed to the changing status of range use and the arrival of many more sheep in Western Colorado. The range had been overstocked with cattle in the early 1880s, and by 1890 there were 100,000 head of cattle grazing on the Western Slope alone. In 1891, the federal government withdrew forest lands from the public domain all over the West. These lands previously had been used as free range for both sheep and cattle. A Congressional resolution followed in 1894, specifically prohibiting the pasturing of all livestock on these Forest Reserves, which were the fore runners of the National Forest System. The result was the closing of much Colorado forest land to livestock—some of which had been sheep range for nomadic herds from Utah and Wyoming. Now the cattlemen's range was potentially shrinking and invading sheep were considered more of a threat than ever.

At the same time, large numbers of sheepmen moved from the diminishing sheep range in Utah and California, pushing their sheep into other states at the same time as public range was decreasing rapidly. At one time cattlemen patrolled much of the Colorado-Utah border in an effort to stop the migration. These border patrol ranchers were armed, determined, short on patience, and short on sleep— not in the mood for sharing. Lines had been drawn, and sheepmen who crossed them experienced the first of the "sheep killings." Cattle ranchers poisoned sheep with strychnine, shot them, dynamited and burned them, and drove them in mass over cliffs to their deaths.

Trouble erupted very early in the San Luis Valley and escalated further in 1880, when large numbers of sheep were brought into the area from New Mexico. Many sheepmen lost their lives over these incidents, so high did the feelings run. Perhaps the San Luis cattle ranchers set an example, for Gunnison County ranchers soon followed suit.

The first of the Gunnison sheep killings occurred in 1901 and is always referred to as the Kezar Basin "incident." A few miles south of Gunnison, a respected local cattleman, who was speculating in the sheep business, brought in a very large herd of sheep by train. His outfit had not been in the country for long when twenty masked men—their horses also masked—surprised the herders, tied and gagged them, and proceeded to bludgeon to death 1,000 to 2,000 sheep. There was hope among the local cattlemen, although steadfastly denying any involvement, that the Kezar Basin incident would be the last act of violence needed—the grim lesson had been learned and would not have to be repeated.

But the summer of 1904 brought temptation again, in the form of plentiful grass in the Taylor Park area. Even knowing they were courting trouble, the hated migratory sheepmen could not resist the vast reaches of grass growing in the park—surely there was enough to go around. A Utah sheep baron moved his flock of approximately 5,000 sheep into the north end of the park. He was not welcomed warmly, especially after indicating that he was prepared to bring in thousands more sheep if he was not met with trouble from the cattlemen that summer. However, trouble found him instead, and very quickly. One hundred masked men, armed with green aspen clubs and rifles, ran about 1,500 sheep into a corral where they were clubbed and shot to death.

The last of Gunnison's sheep killings occurred on July 4, 1918, near Crested Butte. A band of 1,000 sheep was descended upon by three armed men. The sheep herder was tied up and the sheep run over a low cliff. Many of the sheep were injured and

seventy-five were killed. The suspected local cattlemen all seemed to have convenient alibis, and if
outside "help" was involved, no one ever discovered
who it might be.

By far the most tragic of the sheep killing events
occurred near Parachute, (in Garfield County) in
September of 1894. Newspapers reported that sheepmen, who had a claim to certain ranges in that area,
let down their guard one day when several herders
left camp to attend nearby Grand Junction's Peach
Day Festival. In their absence, a number of masked
cowboys arrived at the sheep camp and overpowered the remaining herders. They then proceeded
to stampede nearly 4,000 sheep over the nearly per-
pendicular walls of the Book Cliffs. The fall of some
1,000 feet left dead, bloody sheep scattered out in all
directions.

Delta County's cattlemen had their major confrontation with sheep herders in March of 1916 in
Escalante Canyon. Earlier, there had been minor
skirmishes over sheep and cattle territory, but a
tentative agreement had developed out of the conflicts—sheep would stay on the north side of the
Gunnison River. It was understood that the south
side of the river and, in fact, the whole back side
of the Uncompahgre Plateau belonged to the local
cattlemen by virtue of unwritten law. One courageous sheepman finally decided to challenge this
concept. He even had the audacity to build a "sheep
bridge" across the Gunnison. It was about 100 feet
long and swung on cables high above the river. Upon
its completion, a great number of "woolies" crossed
successfully to the other side. They poured out onto
cattle range, where it was felt that if they stayed, the

local cattle would soon be coming up pretty short on grass. Several Escalante Canyon ranchmen made a night "visit" and proceeded to reportedly shoot 200 sheep. Still the determined sheepman stayed on. It took a second visit by night raiders before the owner hastily returned what was left of his sheep to the "proper" side of the Gunnison River.

In 1911 an incident occurred in northwest Colorado on the Yampa River east of Craig. Here George and Charles Woolley operated a substantial cattle ranch. They were successful in the cattle business, and George served as a Routt County commissioner. Local cattlemen were opposed to sheep coming into the area and had passed resolutions against them at their association meetings. It was therefore somewhat surprising that the Woolleys decided to expand their ranching operation to include the raising of sheep.

The Woolleys had around 100 sheep corralled near their barn on a December night in 1911. Sometime during the night, five riders approached the ranch, cut the phone lines, and slaughtered all the sheep. Attempts to find the killers failed. Shortly after the incident, the pioneer Woolley family left the Craig area and relocated on the eastern slope. There they resumed raising sheep.

Ironically, only a few years after these bloody "sheep wars," a severe drop in cattle prices and a rise in the sheep market caused a few cattlemen and former sheep haters to go into the sheep business. In fact sheep may have been a saving grace for many of the hard pressed cattlemen prior to World War I. One lasting impact of the sheep and cattle conflicts throughout the West was that the stricter regulations and boundaries helped curtail the abuse of range-lands caused by overuse by both sheep and cattle. Certainly the competition between the sheepmen and cattlemen was a precursor of the conflicts to come among the many and varied users of public lands.

CHAPTER 17

Murder of Sheriff Dunlap

LAWMAN'S LAST GOOD DEED

ontezuma County Sheriff Wesley Dunlap, a seasoned, older peace officer, died in the line of duty. He was shot at point-blank range by prisoners that he was transporting from Glenwood Springs to the scene of their crime in Montezuma County. The event took place in 1935 in the canyon of the San Miguel River about nine miles west of Placerville on Highway 145. Placerville is located in the southwestern part of Colorado on the route of the San Juan Skyway, a scenic 236 mile loop that transverses the heart of the San Juan Mountains.

What led to the murder of the sheriff was somewhat complicated. In Montezuma County, in an isolated cabin, lived an elderly sheepman named Jim Westfall. Here, he had lived alone for nearly a quarter of a century. Because of his isolation, no one noticed when he first went missing. When neighbors finally did check on him, they found him dead. He had been gagged, his ankles and wrists bound, and his cabin had been ransacked.

The neighbors who found Westfall's body immediately went for help and returned with the local law enforcement officials. They concluded that a robbery and murder had taken place, and that after the killer or killers had gagged and bound Westfall they had left him to die alone in agony from starvation and exposure. The man had been dead for two or three weeks and whoever had killed him was by now, no doubt, far away.

The two outlaws who had committed the murder were brothers, Otis and Herbert McDaniels. They made the mistake of exhibiting very suspicious behavior after the crime, evidently even bragging about it, and subsequently they were apprehended and placed in the jail in Cortez. A lynching party was promptly organized, so it was decided that the prisoners must be moved to another location. They were taken to Glenwood Springs, located some 200 miles away. The prison walls were stouter there and feelings were not running quite so high.

Three months later, after feelings had died down somewhat, Sheriff Dunlap and a deputy traveled to Glenwood Springs to retrieve the prisoners. The older of the two brothers, Otis, was considered very dangerous—a seasoned criminal. The brothers were to be transported back to Cortez in the sheriff's car, handcuffed, and with their hands and legs shackled together. All went well until the four reached the San Miguel Canyon just outside of Placerville. There, the sheriff saw a car that was overturned and in a ditch, and he left his deputy and the prisoners in the patrol car to see if any help was needed. It was to be his last good deed. As he walked away from his car, the deputy was momentarily distracted, and Otis, whose left wrist was cuffed to the right wrist of his younger brother, used his free hand to retrieve the sheriff's revolver from a pocket in the car door. Otis ordered the deputy out of the car at gunpoint. Herbert then grabbed the sheriff's shotgun. Dunlap saw what had happened and walked back to the car claiming that he would turn the prisoners loose. At a distance of three feet, Otis gunned down the sheriff in cold blood as he pleaded for his life. The prisoners allowed the unarmed deputy to live and made their escape in the car. Medical help was quickly summoned but the sheriff died in an ambulance on the way to nearby Telluride.

A large posse was raised and the surrounding area became the location of a huge manhunt, which included National Guard planes and an army of 500 men who searched over the rugged countryside. Blood hounds from the Colorado State Penitentiary were even brought in. However, five or six days passed and the outlaws were still on the loose. Eventually, it was concluded that they had made a clean get away.

Two more weeks passed before the brothers were finally apprehended twenty miles west of Cañon City, which was about 300 miles from the murder. Two trials took place; at the first, the brothers were found guilty of the murder of Jim Westfall. Charges were then filed in San Miguel County for the slaying of Sheriff Dunlap, and both brothers were also found guilty of this crime. Herbert was sentenced to life in prison and Otis was sentenced to death in the gas chamber at Cañon City.

CHAPTER 18

Delta's Bungled Bank Robbery

❧ WHEN CRIME DOESN'T PAY ❧

The small town of Delta, on the Western Slope of Colorado, is situated forty miles south of Grand Junction at the southwest end of Grand Mesa. The town had barely come into existence and was still in its rough, frontier period when the infamous McCarty gang, known for their bank robbing skills, came to call. Delta's Main Street at this time sported boardwalks and a fairly posh hotel. Churches and schools were being built; still, at this time it was just a "one-horse town" and not at all the place one might think would be picked for a bank robbery—especially by such long time professionals as the McCartys.

The notorious McCarty gang, which operated in several states, had a long history of cattle rustling and bank and train robberies—mostly successful ones. Led by Tom, the oldest of the three McCarty brothers, the outlaw band eventually included such notables as the infamous Matt Warner and Butch Cassidy. The McCarty gang had been working at their lucrative profession for several years when, in 1893, they arrived in Delta. They were alleged to have previously robbed Denver's First National Bank in 1889, and the San Miguel National Bank in Telluride the same year, where they left the town on fast horses with approximately $21,000 of stolen cash. Moving on to Oregon in 1891, they held up several banks, getting away with smaller amounts of money, but never-the-less getting away.

By 1893, with their reputation well-established, they sized up the Farmer's and Merchant's Bank in Delta, as their next mark. Just prior to the robbery they had been holed up at a place called "Robbers Roost," which was located in the maze of canyons between the west side of the Uncompahgre Plateau and Hanksville, Utah. There they laid out their plans for the Delta bank robbery, and what they mistakenly thought would be just a small-time job in a two-bit town. Since some of their more notorious and experienced members were busy elsewhere, it was left to Tom McCarty and his brother Bill to knock off Delta's bank by themselves. The job required three people, however, so they included Bill's son Fred, who was only in his late teens and inexperienced but eager to begin the career that had been so successful for his father and uncle. He had no idea, as he warmed to their developing plan, that the day of the robbery would be the last day of his life.

The McCarty's strategy was quite similar to the one that worked for most experienced bank robbers. The gang owned incredibly fast "get-away" horses, which they had trained to remain calm around gunfire. They also had carefully sized up the town of Delta and its surrounding terrain, picking their escape routes carefully. Unnoticed, they had also appraised the layout of the bank's interior.

On the day of the robbery, all initially went as planned. Their fast mounts were tied behind the Main Street bank, ready for a speedy get-away. The most experienced member of the gang, Tom McCarty, waited in the alley while the other two sauntered into the bank and demanded money at gun point. From there on everything should have been as easy as a Sunday picnic—all that was left was to get out of town fast.

Then everything went wrong. The McCartys hadn't counted on the inexperienced and unskilled Fred losing his cool and becoming "trigger happy." And they surely hadn't counted on a nearby businessman being such a dead shot. When the McCartys went into the bank and made their demands for cash, a clerk reached for something under his desk, possibly a weapon, and young Fred panicked and fired twice, missing the bank employee with the first shot but killing him with the second. The loud shots blew the McCartys' cover, and the frazzled team raced out the back of the bank to the waiting horses. But Tom McCarty, who stood by outside with the horses, wasn't waiting. Upon hearing the shots, he quickly sized up the situation, mounted his horse, and tore out of Delta, heading for a crossing of the Gunnison River north of town. Pounding through the dust on his exhausted horse, he reached the gang's relay horses well ahead of his pursuers and raced on out of the country. Bill and Fred made a gallant effort to follow, but weren't quite quick enough.

Nearby was hardware store owner, Ray Simpson, a thirty-one year old, businessman who was also a superb marksman. That day he had a Sharps rifle within his reach, and the tall, slim, and well-dressed businessman quietly stepped outside with his rifle when he heard gunshots. Knowing what they meant, he immediately assessed the situation. He took aim, not hesitating a moment, and blew off the top of Bill McCarty's head as his horse galloped a half a block away down the alley at full-speed. A few seconds later Bill's ill-fated son, by now even farther away, was also hit in the head by the same cool-headed gunman's rifle shot. Father and son both died at the scene.

The town mourned the loss of the dead bank employee, who was the father of several young children, but the irate citizens wasted no time mourning the dead McCartys. They were propped against a wall and photographed. Bill's horrific head wound was covered with a hat. The resemblance between father and son in the photos is very noticeable, each having dark hair, heavy eyebrows, and looking fit . . . rather fine actually, considering the circumstances. They were then unceremoniously buried in the Potter's Field in the city's cemetery, allegedly in the same box. Their gruesome pictures are still available in the town's museum—a reminder that crime doesn't always pay.

Town hero, Ray Simpson, was given a cash reward for his deed, but he suffered severe emotional aftereffects in spite of the accolades. For some time afterwards, the enraged Tom McCarty, his career cut short, sent threatening letters to Simpson. The hardware store owner subsequently left the state.

*Bill McCarty
after the Delta
bank robbery.
Because the
top of his head
was shot off, a
hat was used
to cover the
damage.*
Photo courtesy
of Delta County
Historical
Society.

*Fred McCarty
photographed
after the Delta
Bank Robbery.*
Photo courtesy
of Delta County
Historical
Society.

There were rumors that Tom McCarty was hiding out on a mesa above LaSal Creek in the western end of Montrose County—relatives and friends were supposedly supplying him grub. Perhaps Simpson didn't want to take any chances.

All is quiet now in Delta's peaceful, pretty cemetery where three victims of the same tragic event rest in peace, buried not far from one another.

(Parts of this story were previously published in *The Fence Post* — Western Slope Edition)

CHAPTER 19

Early-Day Law Enforcement in Grand Junction

❧ CRIME GROWS ALONG WITH THE TOWN ❧

G rand Junction, Colorado is 250 miles west and southwest of Denver. It is located at the junction of the Gunnison and Colorado Rivers and sits in a thirty mile wide valley known as the Grand Valley. It is an attractive town surrounded by unique scenery. To the southwest is the Colorado National Monument, a series of canyons, mesas, and spires that rise up to 500 feet high. To the east, at an elevation of 10,000, feet is Grand Mesa, the largest flat-topped mountain in the world. To the northwest are the Book Cliffs, whose name comes from its cliffs of sandstone that appear similar to a shelf of books.

Law enforcement in early-day Grand Junction first began, as it did in most frontier towns, with the presence of just a single marshal. Then the town's businesses rapidly increased in number and the Denver and Rio Grande Railroad began bringing in passengers and crew. It became a thriving place, and as the town's population grew, so gradually did the number of criminals and peace officers.

Ordinances had to be developed to deal with the problems that began cropping up as soon as the town became more populated and organized. Loose animals seemed to present problems, and stray livestock had to be rounded up, impounded, and advertised as missing. Stray dogs were a big problem, as was the disposal of garbage. The flow of horse and

A Grand Junction Marshal patrolling an early-day parade in downtown Grand Junction.
Photo courtesy of the Museum of Western Colorado.

buggy traffic on the streets had to be controlled, and a law was passed that horse-drawn wagons were to go no faster than six miles per hour.

Jeff Stratton in *An Early History of Western Law Enforcement — The Grand Junction, Colorado Police Department (1882-1930)*, gives us these, along with other, examples of early-day ordinances:

The prohibiting of bawdy houses and houses of ill fame.
The prohibition of appearing in any public place in a state of nudity.
The prohibition of any public sport or exercise likely to scare horses.

The first law enforcement officer in Grand Junction was Marshal James Davis who served from 1882 to 1883. His salary was minimal, and he was described as "a nervy man not afraid to use deadly force with a Colt .45 six shooter." He used thumb cuffs, also called "rippers," and heavy handcuffs and leg irons to control prisoners. His job also consisted of a lot of paperwork, such as serving tax notices or collecting license fees.

Grand Junction's early-day marshals did not lack for business. There were plenty of gambling establishments, houses of prostitution, and general crime to keep them busy. Up until 1917, they patrolled the streets on horseback. One of the police department's engraved saddles from these by-gone days can be seen at the Museum of Western Colorado.

Fritz Becker, a veteran of the police department with twenty-five years on the force, recorded his memories of earlier times in an oral history. He recalled that when trouble was reported to the police department and an officer was needed, the man on desk duty would call the central telephone operator. At night she would switch on a red light on the top of the 1st National Bank. If an officer was out walking his beat he would keep tabs on the light. If it was on, he would go to the nearest telephone (usually at the closest open business) and call to find out what the trouble was and where it was located.

A train robbery caused some excitement near Grand Junction on November 3, 1887. The Salt Lake passenger train on the Denver and Rio Grande Railroad was held up and robbed in the early hours of the morning. Rocks and ties were laid on the track some five miles east of Grand Junction. When the train came to a halt, masked men held the engineer and fireman at gun point and robbed the mail, express, and baggage cars. Because nobody on the train knew the combination to the safe, the robbers disappeared into the night with only $150 in cash. It was rumored that the train was held up by Butch Cassidy, Tom McCarty and Matt Warner. These three would later successfully rob the San Miguel Valley Bank in Telluride.

In 1885 an incident occurred in the Grand Junction jail that left the jailer seriously injured. The jailer was attempting to handcuff two inmates when they somehow got the better of him. One of the inmates had a bottle with which he smashed the jailer over the head. His face was sliced open and the jailer lost consciousness momentarily. When he revived, he went to a nearby house for help with blood running down his face. The two prisoners escaped but were captured later.

Methods such as patrolling on horseback and being signaled by a red light on the top of a bank are, of course, long obsolete. More than a century later, about the only things that the first and the current police departments have in common are dealing with lawlessness on a pretty regular basis.

CHAPTER 20

Lake City Lynching

MURDERERS HUNG FROM THE BRIDGE

he beautiful Lake City area in the San Juan Mountains has a backdrop of five spectacular 14,000 foot peaks. Steep terrain and narrow deep canyons comprise much of its land. The main river is the Lake Fork of the Gunnison, which passes through Lake San Cristobal en route to the Gunnison River. Residents of Lake City are heir to some of the grandest scenery in Colorado.

Beautiful though its setting may have been, in its earliest days as a busy mining camp Lake City was anything but peaceful. The jail was often filled to capacity, and the docket of criminal cases included murder, rape, larceny, assault and battery, and forgery. Street brawls and other troubles were quite common.

On a day late in April of 1882, the Hinsdale County Court House flag flew at half-mast and all of

Lake City's public buildings were draped in black. The town was in mourning for Sheriff E.N. Campbell who had been shot down in the line of duty. Sheriff Campbell had been elected in 1879 to deal with Lake City's law enforcement problems. He was a highly respected and well liked peace officer—a family man with six children.

On April 26th, Sheriff Campbell was gunned down while investigating a robbery and died at the scene. The two thieves who were involved in the robbery, George Betts and James Browning, were local men—partners who owned a brothel and the ill-famed San Juan Central dance hall and saloon, both located on Bluff Street. Betts and Browning were also suspected to be thieves.

A local citizen had reported to the sheriff that he feared Betts and Browning had targeted his vacant but furnished house. The two were suspected of stealing some valuable articles, and it was suspicioned that they would return for more. Sheriff Campbell and Marshal Clair Smith waited in a dark hall of the vacant house one day, hoping to catch the two thieves. Sure enough, the burglars showed up. The two men entered the house and struck a match to see better and thereby revealed their identity to the waiting law enforcement officers. Sheriff Campbell ordered them to drop their guns and throw up their hands. Betts then fired his gun and a fatal bullet struck Sheriff Campbell. Marshal Smith was able to identify Betts and Browning, and they were soon apprehended. Betts was carrying a .44-caliber revolver with one spent cartridge. The bullet that had killed Campbell was a .44. Browning was arrested at the dance hall and charged with being an accessory to the murder.

After the arrests, many of Lake City's residents, who were enraged at the death of the popular sheriff, congregated near the fallen peace officer's home the next day. They were masked and armed with rifles, ropes, and sledge hammers to use to batter down the jail door. They were obviously bent on a lynching, and the guards at the jail didn't make a serious attempt to stop them. Betts and Browning were led to a bridge north of Lake City, where they were both promptly hung. Ropes were thrown over the upper cross beams of the bridge and Betts and Browning were pulled and jerked all the way up, where they strangled to death. It was said that before the hanging young Browning begged for his life, the older Betts only asked for a "chew."

The criminals' bodies were left on display until the next morning, allowing the townsfolk, including children, to view them hanging from the beams of the bridge. The two were finally buried, and the incident was closed with a note in the local newspaper that thoroughly endorsed the hanging.

CHAPTER 21

Violence Visits Telluride and Crested Butte

STRIKING MINERS, SHERIFFS, AND THE STATE MILITIA

O ne would never know it now by looking at the quaint but commercialized ski towns of Telluride and Crested Butte; but once, aside from the spectacular local scenery, these villages were rather sordid and rough mining towns. Each of them was, for a time, rocked by threats of violence—the results of mine strikes. Both early-day Telluride and Crested Butte were mainly inhabited by miners—many of them immigrants. These men were heavily exploited by the mine owners and usually worked mind-numbingly long hours under very unsafe conditions. The result was often injuries and, not infrequently, casualties. The new towns had roughly laid out streets with shacks lining both sides. These flimsy, wooden residences that many miners lived in, were easy prey for fire, sometimes avalanches, and in the winter didn't offer much protection from the bitter cold. Because of such conditions, strikes and confrontations with the mine owners were inevitable. When these "rebellions" happened, the mine owners would attempt to bring in replacement workers (called "scabs"), but violence was often incited against the scabs by the striking miners. Such situations, ripe with high emotion and gang mentality, were recipes for disaster.

Such a cauldron of circumstances boiled over in Crested Butte in 1891. The Colorado Coal and Iron Company operated underground coal mines in the area and employed many miners. Two-hundred and fifty of them went on strike after being told they would be given pay cuts. The angry men began their protests by cutting off the exhaust fans in the mine and allowing the mine chambers to fill with explosive gasses. It was an equally explosive situation above the ground where feelings ran high. Into this setting walked just the right man—a law enforcement officer deemed by one high official to be "a man worth an army" a man with the unmovable presence, strength, and the coolness of an iceberg—Gunnison County's Sheriff Doc Shores. He had been called upon by the Crested Butte mayor and other concerned citizens to try and keep disaster at bay. Shores took the challenge, even though he had earlier been threatened by the striking miners, who said that they would "cut off his head and carry it on a pole in front of a parade" if he tried to interfere.

Shores, who had promised the miners that he would not interfere with the strike as long as there was no trouble, shifted gears when news arrived of the miners shutting off the exhaust fans. He sensed an impending disaster. With twenty-four emergency deputies, including the Marlow brothers who have been previously mentioned, a Catholic priest, and a few mine officials, Doc quietly slipped out of Gunnison by train and arrived in Crested Butte about midnight, hoping that the train (which had its lights turned off) would go unobserved. But word had gotten to Crested Butte ahead of Doc, and he and his deputies were met by 150 miners armed to the teeth and looking for blood.

Doc ordered his posse to quickly vacate the train and immediately drop down behind the slope of the grade where the tracks ran. He instructed them not to shoot unless ordered to, and then to "shoot low" which they eventually were forced to do, wounding thirty-six approaching miners. The miners, sensing that they were outmatched, quickly gave up and retreated. The mine fans were repaired and the town was saved the prospect of a disastrous explosion. The dramatic shoot-out had been one thing, the weather was another. It was twenty below zero that night, and the sheriff and his deputies nearly froze to death on the unheated train before food and blankets were eventually provided.

The next morning, Shores and four of his deputies boldly marched down the town's frozen main street. With them were five mine officials all headed for a conference with the striking miners. Doc and his men were wearing two six- shooters each, the four deputies were also carrying Winchesters. A confrontation followed wherein there were several stormy sessions between lawmen, mine officials, and miners, but which brought about an uneasy truce. The dispute was eventually resolved—most of the parties involved realizing that potential disaster had been prevented by the calm, cool audacity of Sheriff Doc Shores.

Sheriff C.W. (Doc) Shores as he appeared at the time of the Crested Butte mine strike. Faded photograph on the wall of the Gunnison County Sheriff's office.
Walt Barron photo.

Doc Shore's headstone in the Gunnison Cemetery.
Walt Barron photo.

A similar event took place in Telluride, Colorado, a few years later, but it took quite a few more men to quell the violence than it did in the Crested Butte conflict. Telluride was a hard rock mining camp that had come into being in the late 1870s. It is a beautiful, isolated place located near the head of the San Miguel River Valley in the midst of some of Colorado's most rugged mountains. With the discovery of major deposits of ore in the Telluride region, gold mining had developed rapidly and a town had sprung up.

Early on, it was hard for the mine owners in the Telluride area to make a profit, as the first ore brought out of the mountains had to be transported by mule, burro, or wagon for about a hundred miles. A saving grace was the coming of the Rio Grande Southern Railroad in 1890. The ore could now be more inexpensively shipped out of the mountains by rail, and the result was that mining in the area boomed. Legendary mines such as the Tomboy, Smuggler-Union, and Sheridan, allowed their owners to become fabulously rich, living in comfort in elaborate Victorian homes. New money bought such amenities as oak stair cases, parquet floors, stained glass windows, and fancy wood filigree.

Life was a bit different for Telluride's miners, who usually lived in rough boarding houses built on the steep slopes of the nearby mountains or in cold, drafty shacks in town. The miners earned three dollars a day. This amount figured out to less if one took into account the inflated prices at the company store and boarding costs. The men worked in mines far below the surface of the earth, digging tunnels into the steep mountain sides. The mines often operated twenty-four hours a day and ten to twelve hour shifts were the norm. In the dead of winter, snow buried everything, including the paths to town. Isolated miners frequently found themselves out of provisions and had to buy them from the company store, putting them perpetually in debt. Working conditions in the mines were wretched. Many a miner met his fate in one of several unexpected ways: dynamite mishaps, gas buildups, cave-ins, and falls. Outside of the mine, avalanches posed a constant threat, as did such health problems as consumption, black lung, and pneumonia. Deaths were common and most of the men who died were young. Telluride, especially, had an unusually high percentage of widows and orphans who were often left in a state of destitution.

The hard pressed miners agreed that their situation justified the establishment of a union. The Western Federation of Miners chartered a local union in Telluride in 1896. The miners then began to bargain and strike for better pay, better working hours, and less dangerous conditions. For the next few years a succession of altercations occurred between mine owners and miners. The miners went on strikes and the strikes led to the hiring of scabs. Violence between the two factions often resulted. In further retaliation, fires were sometimes started by miners, with mine tunnels and boarding houses being destroyed. Men on both sides died. The only results of this violence seemed to be a continued deadlock in negotiations and more violence. The strikebreakers may have gotten the worst of it. They were disarmed, beaten, and run out of the valley by union members. Union agitators and sympathizers were also at one point literally railroaded out of town as well.

With seemingly no end to the animosity, the state militia was eventually brought in. Martial law was declared in Telluride by Colorado's Governor James H. Peabody. Six railroad carloads of state militia men and a Gatling gun were sent to the devastated little town. Meetings were banned, a curfew was put into place, and saloons were closed. Strikers were loaded like cattle onto the train, sent to Ridgway, and warned not to return. Many did, however, and the feud continued until November of 1904, when the miners' union recognized its inevitable defeat, with most of its demands ultimately being rejected. The mine owners as well as the town's shop keepers and businessmen, knowing they had the backing of the militia, won out in the end. It would be many more years before conditions improved for the miners in any significant way.

And so the Crested Butte and Telluride mining disputes were finally settled, perhaps not in an entirely fair way to all concerned, but at least peace reigned again and business could at last go on as usual. Both towns eventually became sleepy little mining villages until the twentieth century when a thing called "skiing" woke the two sleeping giants.

(A relic of this unsettling time remains in the Telluride area and can be visited today. There is a small rock structure at the summit of Imogene Pass, between Telluride and Ouray. It was erected in 1904 as a fort for the militiamen who were stationed there to prevent union activists from reentering the area over the pass. It was referred to as "Ft. Peabody" in reference to the governor's role in breaking the union.)

CHAPTER 22

Meeker's Bungled Bank Robbery

SPEEDY DISPOSAL OF BANK ROBBERS

Meeker is located in northwestern Colorado in the heart of the White River Valley. It is a quaint, beautiful little town situated near both the Routt and the White River National Forests. Meeker is located in a wide fertile valley and has always been largely an agricultural and ranching community.

On an October afternoon in 1896, the sleepy little town of Meeker came wide awake when it became the location of a bank robbery. This hold-up was bungled even more seriously than the one by the McCartys in Delta, Colorado, three years earlier. If outlaws were inclined to learn anything from prior unsuccessful bank robberies, then George Law, Jim Shirley, and "The Kid" Pierce, (alias "The Kid" Smith) were slow learners indeed.

The three men, who had recently come to town from Brown's Park, rode into Meeker on one fall afternoon, casually tied up their horses, and then strode to the Hugus building—a bank and general store on Main Street. They entered this establishment with guns drawn, stationing themselves at the rear door, the front door, and the cashier's window. No sooner had they arrived, so full of confidence and bravado, than things began to go wrong. George Law, the more mature and seasoned of the lot, stepped up to the cashier's window and fired a couple of shots to show that he meant business. The manager of the building and several clerks looked up to find they were covered by Jim Shirley, who had been stationed at the back door. At that point, several customers and the employees of the store and bank were ordered to put up their hands.

George Law's two shots alerted the townspeople that the bank was being robbed; and just about all of Meeker's able-bodied men immediately came to the scene—every corner and every door was guarded by wary citizens bent on upholding law and order in Meeker.

By that time the robbers had taken a few hundred dollars from the cash drawer and put it into a sugar sack. As they started out a side door of the building, they herded several hostages in front of them. When the outlaws reached the street, they became aware of the awaiting mob and proceeded to march the hostages to where the horses were tied. One of the hostages chose that moment to run and the situation started to quickly unravel. The remaining hostages all scattered. Then the shooting began, with three of the hostages being injured by the robbers in the confusion. The townsmen returned fire, and Jim Shirley and "The Kid" were shot down immediately. George Law attempted to run, but two bullets also brought him down. He died an hour later, allegedly calling for his mother.

The three dead robbers were photographed in the gruesome manner of the day, hands folded over their breasts, two with their eyes open, the third with a death grimace. They went to their just reward having left the sugar sack of money behind in the bank in all the excitement.

The outlaws were buried in Meeker's Highland Cemetery, their graves marked by three small identical slabs lying flat in the grass. Here they sleep, perhaps even peacefully, while a century later, on some occasions such as the Fourth of July, the

"The Kid," Jim Shirley, and George Law (alias George Harris) shown after being shot down during the Meeker bank robbery.

Photo courtesy of the White River Museum.

∽

townspeople of Meeker reenact their crime for the
enjoyment of the tourists.

(Parts of this article were previously published
in *The Fence Post* — Western Slope Edition)

CHAPTER 23

The Wildest of the "Wild Bunch"
"KID CURRY"

He didn't look wild and dangerous. Surviving photographs show a thoughtful, well-groomed gentleman. He looked like a store clerk or the mild-mannered teacher of a one-room school . . . but this he was not. Harvey Logan, alias "Kid Curry," was one of the most notorious, cold-blooded killers ever known to the West. Before his career ended, he had been a member of Butch Cassidy's Wild Bunch, participated in several daring train robberies, had nine murders to his credit, and had become one of the West's most wanted men. He was known to be absolutely fearless and was alleged to have been involved in more robberies and killings than any other outlaw of his time.

Harvey Logan was born in the Midwest shortly after the Civil War. He moved with other family members to the West, eventually ending up in Montana, where he engaged in ranching and raising horses. It is believed that he was a legitimate businessman until around 1894, when he killed a man in a drunken brawl and then fled to the notorious outlaw hang-out, "Hole-in-the-Wall." From that point he began a career in crime that steadily became ever more daring. Along the way, in various scrapes and in various places, he killed a deputy sheriff, rode with the outlaw "Black Jack" Ketchum, robbed a bank in Belle Fourche, South Dakota, and eventually wound up riding with Butch Cassidy.

He was with the Wild Bunch in June of 1899, when they robbed the Union Pacific Railroad near Wilcox, Wyoming, and then he participated in the daring robbery of a Union Pacific train at Tipton, Wyoming. In June of 1900, the gang blew up that train's express car safe and rode off into the night with the loot. After this string of train robberies, the gang was hunted relentlessly by lawmen.

From time to time Harvey Logan enjoyed the companionship of Annie Rogers, a prostitute who was a favorite of the Wild Bunch. Annie would wait patiently for Logan while he rode the outlaw trail. When he returned they would frequent expensive hotels and fancy restaurants. Photos of Annie reveal a small, dark haired, pretty, but serious looking woman.

Logan joined, left, and rejoined the Wild Bunch on several occasions, and, throughout this time, he was constantly pursued by lawmen. Several of them died by Logan's gun, and he always managed to somehow escape and go on to participate in another train robbery . . . the next one a Union Pacific train in Montana. In 1902, he was finally captured, arrested, and convicted of robbery. But he escaped and headed back to his old haunts, eventually coming to Western Colorado, where fate finally caught up with him.

In 1904, continuing on with his successful career of robbing trains, Harvey Logan, or "Kid Curry" as he had become known, staged his last hold-up. Along with two other men, he robbed a Denver and Rio Grande train near today's Parachute, Colorado. After the hold-up, a posse was quickly on the outlaw's trail. Logan was wounded and soon surrounded by lawmen. At this point, when escape looked hopeless, he allegedly took his own life. Thus, on June 7, 1904, he fulfilled the foreboding statement of Western Colorado's famed lawman C.W. "Doc" Shores, who once stated that "those who live by the gun, usually die by the gun, be he peace officer or outlaw."

And so supposedly ended the life of one of the West's most infamous criminals; however, unfounded rumors persisted over the years, that Kid Curry had actually escaped and lived on somewhere in the West.

CHAPTER 24

The Bad Men of Brown's Park

❧ OUTLAW HIDEOUT ❧

B rown's Park is located in the northwest corner of Colorado. It is walled in by mountains and has a wide valley floor below, through which flows the Green River. The park has a mild climate, a treasure trove of plentiful, rich grass, and was ideally located for the early-day fur traders and later day cattle outfits.

Brown's Park is beautiful without a doubt, but tough as nails. Fur traders were the first white men to inhabit the park, but after they left, the cattlemen moved in, and along with them, cattle rustlers, horse thieves, and other outlaws. It was a perfect place for men on the run to "hole up." It was located far off the beaten path and criss-crossed with canyons and arroyos; many caves had been carved out in its sandstone cliffs by the elements. It was a good place to hide and also an easy ride to the border of another state.

The road through the park was part of the "Outlaw Trail." This famous route crossed the states between Canada and Mexico. Outlaws traveled south from the Montana border, across Wyoming, Utah, Colorado, and Arizona and on over to New Mexico, ending up in Texas on the Mexican border. The heyday of the Outlaw Trail was from 1870 to 1910, when a large number of lawless men traveled over it, many coming through Brown's Park. This circumstance helped to label Brown's Park, for a time at least, as one of the most lawless places around. It ranked right up there with Hole-in-the-Wall in Wyoming and Robbers Roost in Utah.

Some frequent visitors to Brown's Park who were mentioned elsewhere in this book, were "Butch Cassidy," Harvey Logan (alias "Kid Curry"), Tom and Bill McCarty, Matt Warner, Tom Horn, Isom Dart, and Harry Longabaugh, alias the "Sundance Kid."

Matt Rash showed up in Brown's Park in the early 1880s, bringing with him a questionable reputation. He worked for a couple of the local cattle outfits before starting his own ranch. He was known to be "tough as a pine knot" but must have had his tender side, too, as it was rumored that he was romancing his neighbor Anne Basset, who would later be known as "Queen Anne of Brown's Park" and also as "Queen of the Cattle Rustlers." It was suspected that Matt Rash was a pretty successful rustler himself. He was warned by a note on his door (probably left there by one of the big cattle outfits) that he should leave the

Matt Rash.
Photo courtesy
of the Museum
of Northwest
Colorado.

country. This he refused to do, and in July of 1900, Matt was found dead in his bed with two bullet holes in his body. The story goes that he tried to write a death message in his own blood . . . perhaps naming his killer. It was believed that, as with Isom Dart, Matt Rash was shot down by "cattle rustler exterminator" Tom Horn.

Along with the bad men of Brown's Park were a few women. Laura Bullion was a prostitute, best known for her association with the Wild Bunch. It is believed that on occasion she rode with them and even participated in one of their robberies. She knew how to use a six shooter and didn't mind the rough outdoor life the men lived. On the other hand, when dressed in expensive gowns, she was said to be a "knockout."

Eventually the outlaws departed, and the Wild West was tamed. Brown's Park, once made such a violent place by desperadoes, is quiet now. By 1965 the valley had evolved into a much different place when it became the location of the Brown's Park National Wildlife Refuge, designated as a habitat for migratory waterfowl. Its purpose is to provide sanctuary for migratory birds, protect natural resources, conserve endangered and threatened species, and to offer fish and wildlife-dependent recreational opportunities. Its wildlife, beauty, cultural heritage, and its lawless past make Brown's Park an interesting place indeed.

CHAPTER 25

Neck Tie Parties

QUICK JUSTICE

I n the early days of the West, from the gold rush era to the early 1900s, lynching was the prevalent method of disposing of outlaws on Colorado's Western Slope. An 1880s Lake City poster even warned would-be criminals of that very real possibility. A vigilante group in Lake City devised the notice and posted it around town warning "thieves, dance-house loungers and foot-pads" to either get out of town or face the noose. A large black coffin adorned the poster in order to give it special emphasis.

It was certainly not uncommon on the Western Slope for citizens to band together in vigilance groups when they thought it necessary. If they felt local law enforcement was ineffective, or if it was lacking entirely, vigilantes took the law into their own hands, and a lynching was often the result. Their methods of justice ranged from engaging a "hired gun" to do the deed or doing it themselves. Vigilante justice could take the form of beating, branding, shooting, or hanging an alleged offender.

Such groups were, of course, acting under the pretext of upholding law and order; even though, for the most part, they were acting illegally themselves. Sometimes a town's vigilance committee was established prior to a crime being committed, but often it took the form of an impromptu mob . . . unorganized and angry people bent on vengeance.

Stephen J. Leonard, in his book, *Lynching in Colorado*, claims that 175 lynchings took place in Colorado from 1859 to 1919. He states, "Judge Lynch prowled Colorado like a wolf until 1903, after which he rarely found a victim."

The targets for lynch mobs were usually thieves of one type or another . . . cattle rustlers or horse thieves being the most common. Also often targeted were murderers and rapists. Considered especially serious was horse theft, and some territorial laws even authorized the lynching of a horse thief. In all these cases the lynch mob did not bother to firmly establish the victim's guilt but served as prosecutor, judge, jury, and executioner. The crime committed may have indeed been real; but it may also have only been suspected, or even just anticipated.

To get to their victim, a mob of vigilantes sometimes had to bypass what law and order had already been established—break into a jail, over-power a jailer, and take the prisoner by force. Such mobs might be comprised of any combination of types of people and often included some of the community's more solid citizens.

Of course, the hangings of criminals after a trial were legal, but they were also quick. In Durango on May 23, 1882, a man named Bill Woods shot an unarmed customer in a saloon. Woods was arrested, tried, and found guilty of premeditated murder. He was sentenced to be hanged. A month after the shooting had occurred, on June 23, the execution took place at noon and was witnessed by 300 people, including women and children.

After a lynching victim was secured, punishment was usually very swift and merciless. In the case of hangings, a noose might be quickly fashioned and the victim was strung up from the beam of a bridge or a barn rafter . . . or more likely a tree branch. People who were hanged were supposed to have their neck broken, causing instant death, but victims were often hung incorrectly and died a slow death by strangulation. A lynching victim in Silverton, who was placed standing on a chair while a noose was placed around his neck, allegedly became impatient with the process. He said, "adios, gentlemen" and kicked the chair out from under himself.

Besides lynching there were also some terrible cases where the victim was burned alive. After a lynching, the corpse was sometimes left hanging for a time to serve as a warning to others. Often a note was pinned to the shirt branding the offender as a murderer or a horse thief. One note in Durango read "He who takes me down will suffer the same fate."

According to Stephen J. Leonard, "Lynching flourished in Colorado . . . few towns of any size went without at least one lynching." The Western Slope towns were no exception with lynchings taking place in Ouray, Durango, Lake City, Silverton, Gunnison and many other towns.

CHAPTER 26

The Many Marshals of Tin Cup

❧ TRIPS TO BOOT HILL ❧

T in Cup, Colorado, was a tough place to be a town marshal in the early 1880s. In fact, the little high-altitude mining camp went through eight of them before the town was even dry behind the ears.

Tin Cup is located forty-seven miles northeast of Gunnison and three miles due west of the Continental Divide. The town supposedly got its name from an early prospector who once filled his cup with water and gravel from a stream and discovered gold.

Tin Cup boomed after the discovery of gold, and the town's population quickly grew to around 5,000—possibly even more. Keeping up with the rapid growth in population was an increase in lawlessness. The town passed ordinances and appointed marshals to try to keep things under control, but in the early 1880s none of the marshals seemed to last very long. It was said that at one time a group of thugs called the "Black Hills Gang" actually controlled Tin Cup, "running" the mayor, town council, and the marshals. Of the eight marshals appointed in the early years: two quit, one was fired, three were gunned down, and one went insane. The eighth marshal actually finished out his term of office.

One of the early marshals appointed in Tin Cup was F.B. Wells. He was informed by the thugs who ran the town that the first man he attempted to arrest would be his last. All that the Black Hills Gang wanted was an appearance of orderliness in the town, so that new residents would not be discouraged to locate there. Marshal Wells never arrested a man during his tenure in Tin Cup.

When Marshal Harry Rivers was appointed, the residents were becoming tired of the rule of the Black Hills Gang and they encouraged the new marshal to "clean up the town." This he did, faithfully enforcing the law and jailing a number of people. He did not tolerate drunkenness, prostitution, or illegal gambling. In March of 1882, he arrested Charles LaTourette, a saloon keeper with whom he had a long-standing feud. LaTourette was released on bail, returned to his saloon, and confronted Marshal Rivers on the boardwalk. Accounts differ as to who was the first to draw and who was drinking and who was not. But the shoot-out ended with Marshal Rivers being killed by a bullet to the head. LaTourette later appeared in front of a "kangaroo court" in Tin Cup. His case was dismissed because it was found that he had acted in "self defense."

Another Tin Cup marshal, Frank Emerson, after his term of office, became involved in a deadly feud. He and another man accosted each other in front of the Pacific Hotel. Each thought that the other was going to draw, but Emerson was fired on first and was killed instantly, shot through the neck and heart.

Twenty-seven year old Marshal Andy Jamison served from 1882 to 1883 and died in a bar fight on May 6, 1883. He was involved in a saloon brawl with a former friend, William Taylor, at Tin Cup's St. James Hotel. He found himself knocked to the floor, and as he was getting up he was shot and killed by Taylor.

The three marshals who were killed by gunfire are all buried in Tin Cup's unique cemetery located on four knolls. There is a Protestant Knoll, a Catholic

Ancient grave on one of the knolls of Tin Cup's cemetery where three early-day town marshals are buried.

Author's collection.

Knoll, a Jewish Knoll, and a Boot Hill Knoll for those who died by violence. Buried in the Protestant Knoll is Frank Emerson. Buried in the Boot Hill Knoll are Andy Jamison and Harry Rivers.

Now a lonesome wind blows through the pines at the old Tin Cup Cemetery. Few of the graves from over a century ago remain marked, as their wooden head boards weathered away long ago. The once "rip-roaring" town of Tin Cup is now little more than a summer get away with a few tourist cabins. It is totally deserted in the winter.

CHAPTER 27

Cattle Rustling and Quick Justice

🔱 "GET THE ROPE" 🔱

A s can be seen by many of the previous stories in this book, during the early days on the Western Slope of Colorado, cattle rustling existed on a grand scale. It was rampant throughout much of the rest of the West as well. In 1867 the state's cattlemen banded together and formed the Colorado Stock Growers Association. This group of men came into existence for the specific purpose of dealing with widespread and blatant cattle rustling. By 1884 the Stock Growers had formed an alliance with an organization called the "Rocky Mountain Detective Association."

There were many who believed that the twenty-five or so peace officers of this "detective agency" were, in some cases, little more than hired guns—

quite a few of them with past histories that were plenty shady. Whatever the legality or state of affairs of these cattle detectives, they were given a lot of latitude. They could commandeer fresh horses from any ranch, if needed, and travel on any train with a free pass, if they were acting in the line of duty and in pursuit of the lawless. It is recorded that while their detective work was pretty successful, in the end it was not successful enough to turn back the constant influx of new rustlers.

The threat of being sentenced to the state penitentiary or, worse yet, being hanged by an angry mob didn't seem to deter the rustlers much. Those men who were skilled at brand changing and hell bent on cattle thieving seemed to be willing to take their chances. In Western Colorado cattle were frequently kept in very remote places and often were without much supervision. Colorado's Western Slope was simply too immense for angry cattleman or brave lawman to oversee very successfully.

As mentioned before, cattle rustling in the early days was classed by law as grand larceny, but an even more serious crime was horse theft. A man's very life might depend on his horse, and it was considered that there was nothing lower than a man who would steal another man's horse. In the early days, stockmen who had been the victims of cattle rustling or horse theft would often resort to lynching the offenders or, in some cases, evened the score with a gun. It seems that in spite of the actions of heroic sheriffs, sometimes ordinary men felt called upon to take on the role of law enforcers. Without any pretense of a trial, a rustler would be served quick justice "Old West" style.

An example of such action occurred in the early 1920s, when a posse of stockmen and a local sheriff were involved in the capture of horse thieves in the Powderhorn area, which is about thirty miles south of Gunnison. A local youth and his sidekick had unsuccessfully competed for prize money at Gunnison's Cattlemen's Days rodeo, and perhaps they had decided that stealing horses was an easier way to make money. They stole a five-year old mare and a fourteen year old bay from a rancher in Salida and brought the horses over Cochetopa Pass, stopping for the night at a ranch located mid-way to Powderhorn. The pair declined to sell or trade the horses when made a generous offer and something about their demeanor caused suspicion. The pair stated their intention of going on west with the horses. The sheriff in Salida was informed of the pair's dubious activities, and he alerted Sheriff Hanlon in Gunnison, who called upon Powderhorn ranchers for assistance in the form of a posse. The posse consisted of William Perry Sammons, his two sons, and fellow ranchers. They had struck the track of the horse thieves going across a hill south into the Powderhorn Valley. In the breaks of a canyon, the posse caught up with the accused, who were holed up in a cabin.

Sammons determined that the men were asleep by peeking through the window. He was angry. Nothing angered a hard working cattleman so much as a horse thief. The posse was armed and ready for action. "Kick that door down and get out of the way," Sammons ordered. The door was kicked open just as the sleeping youths reached for their guns, but they were too late. Sammons' next order to the posse was, "get the rope," for he meant to hang the thieves on the spot from a beam in the roof of the cabin. His fellow posse members talked him out of the hanging, although it took some doing. Instead, they escorted the thieves and stolen horses into the nearby little town of Spencer to wait for the sheriff. The newspaper described it thus, "a fine sight to see the stockmen with rifles across their saddles and stern faces ride into Spencer that evening, drilling ahead of them the thieves who had been marched in this fashion for ten miles."

This instance served to prove that when there was no law available, or law enforcement was too far away, there was seemingly no need to flinch from serving quick justice to those who were deemed deserving of being hanged on the spot. When an angry cattleman barked out, "get the rope," it wasn't going to be a good day for the outlaw who had branded the wrong maverick or ridden the wrong horse.

(The above story is one handed down from my husband's grandfather, William Perry Sammons.)

CHAPTER 28

Chief Ouray of the Utes

🌿 MURDER PLOTS FOILED 🌿

S ituated south and east of Gunnison is an area called "Cochetopa." The Cochetopa Hills, a range of mountains following the Continental Divide, form the eastern boundary. It also includes Cochetopa Pass (today called "North Pass" on Hwy. 114). Far removed from both the towns of Gunnison and Saguache, this is a very remote area—a country of lofty mountains, gently rolling hills, beautiful open parks, steep canyon walls, and a string of hay meadows that carpet the valley floor.

Historically, the Ute Indians roamed this land. Also located here for a brief time was the first Los Piños Indian Agency. From 1868 to 1873, the Utes had been forced to relinquish the San Luis Valley and to give up valuable mining lands in the San Juans. As more and more white men entered their territory, the Utes found themselves pushed further into Western Colorado. In 1868 they were placed on reservations under the auspices of "agencies"—the White River Agency for the Northern Utes and the Los Piños Agency for the southern tribes.

Murder and treachery didn't just take place among the whites. In the summer of 1868, the Southern Utes began arriving at the Los Piños Agency. Eventually, about a dozen or so buildings were built in a 200-foot quadrangle. There were houses for the agent and other employees, corrals, stables, a school, and a blacksmith shop. The buildings were of log, plastered with mud and whitewashed. Chief Ouray had a small adobe house in one corner of the square.

Ouray had been born in New Mexico, son of a Jicarilla Apache father and a Tabeguache Ute mother. By the time he was an adult, Ouray could speak the Spanish, English, Apache, and Ute languages. At the age of eighteen he moved to what would become Colorado and became a member of the Tabeguache Ute tribe, eventually becoming its chief. As chief he sought peace between the conflicting interests of the Native Americans and the whites. For this he was considered a coward among the more militant sub-chiefs of the Utes, many of whom were also jealous of his position.

Five of these sub-chiefs plotted to murder Ouray at the Los Piños Agency in 1872. Included in this group was his own brother-in-law, Sapovanaro. These five men had hidden in the agency's blacksmith shop and waited for Ouray to bring his horse in to be shod. The blacksmith forewarned Ouray and put him on his

Ouray and Chipeta made a handsome couple but, in this photograph, their faces reflect a troubling time for the Utes.

P. David Smith Collection.

guard, so that when Sapovanaro approached swinging an ax, Ouray was able to duck behind a post. A second blow hit the post and shattered the ax handle. Ouray then lunged at Sapovanaro and pushed him into an irrigation ditch. At this point the other four would-be attackers fled. Ouray's wife Chipeta intervened and grabbed Ouray's knife out of its sheaf, preventing Ouray from using it on her brother and taking his life.

Ouray was not molested for some time after this incident. Later on, however, five other Utes bent on making trouble for Ouray did not benefit from the intervention of Chipeta as had Sapovanaro. Utes named Suckett, Dynamitz, Jack of Clubs, Old Nick, and Mr. Hot Stuff were shot and killed.

According to Sidney Jocknick in *Early Days on the Western Slope of Colorado*, "Ouray's summary method of disposing of his enemies is probably without parallel in the annals of the American Indian."

Upon Chief Ouray's death in 1880 an obituary in *The Denver Tribune* read, "He has figured for many years as the greatest Indian of his time . . . A friend to the white man and protector of the Indians alike."

CHAPTER 29

Paradox Valley Murder

 HIDING IN PARADISE

T he beautiful Paradox Valley, located in south-western Colorado, in western Montrose County, is an isolated region bordered by picturesque rim rock formations on its north and south sides and backed by Utah's La Sal mountains to the west. It is a remote and rugged area named for a unique "paradox" of geography. The Dolores River runs across the midsection of the valley floor, while most rivers flow lengthwise through a valley.

Early-day Paradox was a place of lawlessness. It provided a stopping off place along the famous "Outlaw Trail." Used as an escape route by outlaws on the run, Paradox saw its share of cattle rustlers and robbers. In its early history, wagon trains were sometimes ambushed to keep homesteaders from staking government claims and encroaching on the

free range. Later on, when the valley was more settled, many fights broke out over water.

Two early pioneers to the area were John and
James Prentiss. They arrived in the valley in 1881 and
homesteaded near the confluence of Paradox Creek
and the Dolores River. They steadily made improve-
ments to their homestead, building a cabin and help-
ing build a school. When the neighborhood school
was finished, John was hired as its teacher. He proved
to be a popular and successful school master and was
highly regarded by the parents of the students.

All went well at the homestead and school until
John Prentiss suddenly went missing. Brother James,
when questioned, reported that John had gone to
Chicago. Shortly after that, James turned up missing also. The neighbors became suspicious about the
brothers' abrupt departure, leaving, as they apparently had, during the busy harvest season.

Leery neighbors then searched the Prentiss
place. John was found dead. He had been crammed
into the well and covered up with a mattress, straw,
and barbed wire. He had been shot in the head with
a Winchester rifle, and his head had been bashed in
with a hammer.

James was suspected of the crime and was apprehended trying to board a train in nearby Montrose.
Instead of being returned to his small community,
where feelings were running high and a lynching was
feared, he was sent on to Gunnison to be kept under
the watchful eye of Sheriff Doc Shores.

Investigation into the Prentiss brothers' background turned up some surprising results. The
townspeople were amazed to find that their trusted
neighbors, the Prentiss brothers, were actually ex-

convicts operating under aliases. Their real surname was Wilson. The popular school teacher, in fact, had a price on his head.

James, whose given name was actually Virgil, was eventually returned to Montrose for trial. He was found guilty of murder and sentenced to life in prison at the Cañon City penitentiary. The motive for his crime remains shrouded in mystery.

The Prentiss (Wilson) brothers had sought refuge in the remote Paradox Valley, had successfully obtained safety there, and might have gone on that way had they not turned on each other.

CHAPTER 30

The Man Who Shot Jesse James

❧ BOB FORD ❧

I n the midst of the reign of terror of outlaw Jesse James, Missouri governor Thomas Crittenden offered a $10,000 reward for the infamous outlaw—dead or alive. President Ulysses S. Grant also called for his capture. Jesse then began living under the alias of "Thomas Howard."

At this time, a young man, Robert Ford, stepped forward. As a teen, Ford had been somewhat of an admirer of Jesse James. He finally got to meet Jesse in person in 1880, and later he and his brother Charlie became lesser members of the James-Younger gang. When the reward was offered for James' capture, Ford decided to take advantage of his position and earn the prize. He went so far as to meet with

Governor Crittenden, where plans to kill Jesse James were formulated.

In April of 1882, Bob and Charlie Ford were at James' house having breakfast. Jesse rose, went into the living room, removed his gun belt, and proceeded to get up on a chair to dust off a picture. Bob Ford saw his chance. Jesse was shot in the back of the neck and died instantly. He had been unarmed, with his back to his adversary.

Bob Ford had, of course, expected the $10,000 reward for his actions, not to mention huge amounts of public adulation. Instead he was put on trial for murder and sentenced to hang. He was pardoned by the governor but never did receive the reward money.

The Ford brothers became viewed as traitors and cowards. In two years Charlie committed suicide. Bob tried to make a living by posing for photographs as "the man who killed Jesse James" or by reenacting the murder in traveling shows.

Bob wandered around the West and eventually landed in the silver boom town of Creede, Colorado, with plans to open a saloon. Shortly after, he was run out of town for shooting out windows and street lamps on Creede's Main Street while on a drunken spree. He was eventually allowed to return to the town, where he opened up "Ford's Exchange," a dance hall. Not long after he opened this establishment, it burned to the ground, part of a major fire in downtown Creede. In two days he re-opened his business in a tent.

A day later a man named Edward O'Kelly entered the tent and hailed Bob Ford, whose back was turned. As Ford turned to see who was speaking to him, he was shot with a double barreled shotgun at close range. He died at the scene.

O'Kelly was arrested on the spot by Creede's sheriff and transferred to the Rio Grande County jail to avoid a lynching. At his trial in July of 1892, he pleaded not guilty to second degree murder. He was found guilty and sentenced to life in the state penitentiary in Cañon City. In 1902 he was pardoned. He refused to discuss the shooting and was shot himself two years later in Oklahoma City by a law enforcement officer. His claim to fame in history would be as "the man who shot the man who shot Jesse James."

CHAPTER 31

Telluride Bank Robbery

BUTCH CASSIDY'S FIRST HIT

Outlaw Matt Warner was looking for someone to assist in robbing the bank in Telluride. He chose as his associates Tom McCarty, who would later attempt to rob Delta's bank, and young Bob Leroy Parker, who later became known as "Butch Cassidy." These three rode into town on June 24, 1889, the day after a large sum of money had been sent to Telluride for the mine payroll. The three men were well-dressed and appeared to be auspicious-looking cowboys in town for the day. They entered the bank, a small wood frame building, leaving one man outside to hold the horses. Holding the teller at gunpoint, they quickly rounded up a little over $20,000. Butch Cassidy hastily dumped gold, silver dollars, and bills into a gunny sack. Just as quickly as they had arrived, the three robbers departed the bank and tore out of town, firing a few shots along the way to convince any potential followers that they meant business.

The trio had relay horses stationed along their getaway route about twenty miles south of Telluride and, on these fresh mounts, easily outran the pursuing posse. The posse stopped at the relay point, knowing that with tired horses they had no chance of catching up. It is believed that the method of using relay horses was first introduced at this robbery.

There are conflicting stories recorded about the Telluride bank robbery relay horses. One version states that the first group of relay horses was not reachable because the outlaws had been forced to take a different getaway route. According to this version, horse carcasses were found several months later still tied to trees. A second change of horses had been stationed for use by the robbers between Rico and Dolores.

After Warner, Cassidy, and McCarty traded horses, they rested awhile and then moved on. All three soon left the area. Matt Warner went into Utah. Tom McCarty returned to Paradox where his brother Bill had a ranch. He found a hideout near the ranch, located above La Sal Creek. He spent the winter there. The place was later called "Hideout Mesa." Butch Cassidy eventually returned to Brown's Park.

Telluride's Sheriff Jim Clark, who was known to operate on both sides of the law, was conveniently out of town the day that McCarty, Warner, and Cassidy robbed the bank. It was always suspected that they left his share of the loot under a log in a pre-arranged location. Doc Shores and Jim Clark are examples of lawmen at either end of the spectrum, yet the two men were good friends. As mentioned earlier, Shores even covered up the evidence that his friend Clark was a bandit. Sometimes there was a very fine line between a lawman and the lawless. At other times there was a distinct division between those who lived lives of crime, and those brave and fearless men who attempted to uphold the law in the early days on Colorado's Western Slope.

Bibliography

BOOKS

Anderson, Paul and Johnson, Ken. *Elk Mountain Odyssey*. Carbondale, Colorado: Redstone Press, 1998.

Bartholomew, Ed. *The Bibliographical Album of Western Gunfighters*. Houston: The Frontier Press of Texas, 1958.

Becker, Cynthia S., and Smith, P. David. *Chipeta Queen of the Utes—A Biography*. Montrose, Colorado: Western Reflections Publishing Company, 2003.

1956 Brand Book of the Denver Posse of the Westerners, Number XII. Boulder: Johnson Publishing Company, 1957.

Brockett, D.A., *George Crawford's Attic—Dusting Off Grand Junction, Colorado's Past*. Lake City, Colorado: Western Reflections Publishing Company, 2008.

Burroughs, John. *Where the Old West Stayed Young.* New York: Bonanza Books, 1962.

Buys, Christian J. *Historic Telluride in Rare Photographs.* Ouray, Colorado: Western Reflections, Inc., 1998.

Carhart, Arthur H. "Badman's Last Hang-Out." *The Westerner's Denver Posse—1952 Brand Book.* Denver: Zeuch Printing, 1953.

Carlson, Chip. *Tom Horn—Blood on the Moon—Dark History of the Murderous Cattle Detective.* High Plains Press, 2001.

Churchill, Richard E. *Doc Holiday, Bat Masterson, & Wyatt Earp—Their Colorado Careers.* Montrose, Colorado: Western Reflections Publishing Co., 2005.

De Arment, Robert K. *Bat Masterson—The Man and the Legend.* Norman: University of Oklahoma Press, 1979.

Fetter, Richard L. and Suzanne. *Telluride From Pick to Powder.* Caldwell, Idaho: The Caxon Printers, Ltd., 1892.

Fishell, Dave. *The Grand Heritage: A Photographic History of Grand Junction, Colorado.* Norfolk/ Virginia Beach, Virginia: The Donning Company Publishers, 1985.

Frink, Maurice. *When Grass Was King.* University of Colorado Press, 1956.

Goff Richard, and McCaffree, Robert. *Century in the Saddle.* Colorado Cattlemen's Centennial Commission. Boulder: Johnson Publishing Company, 1967.

Greager, Howard E. *Posey's Spurs.* Ouray, Colorado: Western Reflections, Inc., 1999.

Greager, Howard E. *The Hell That Was Paradox*. Boulder, Colorado: Johnson Printing, 1992.

Gregory, Doris. *History of Ouray—A Heritage of Mining and Everlasting Beauty*. Ouray, Colorado: Cascade Publications, 1995.

Jessen, Kenneth. *Colorado Gunsmoke*. Boulder: Pruett Publishing, 1986.

Jocknick, Sidney. *Early Days on the Western Slope of Colorado*. Glorieta, New Mexico: The Rio Grande Press, Inc., 1968.

Karolevitz, Robert. *Doctors of the Old West*. Seattle, Washington: Superior Publishing Company, 1967.

Leonard, Stephen J. *Lynching in Colorado 1859-1919*. Boulder: University Press of Colorado, 2002.

Look, Al. *Unforgettable Characters of Western Colorado*. Boulder: Pruett Press, Inc., 1966.

Marlow, Charley and Marlow, George. *Life of the Marlows, A True Story of Frontier Life of Early Days—As Related by Themselves*. Ouray, Colorado: *Ouray Harold* Print. Undated.

Marshall, Muriel. *The Awesome 'Dobie Badlands*. Ouray, Colorado: Western Reflections Inc., 2000.

Marshall, Muriel. *Red Hole In Time*. College Station: Texas A&M University Press, 1988.

Marshall, Muriel. *Where Rivers Meet—Lore From the Colorado Frontier*. College Station: Texas A&M University Press, 1996.

McGaughey, Kathryn. *Below the Rimrocks*. Montrose, Colorado: Western Reflections Publishing, 2003.

Melrose, Frances. *Rocky Mountain Memories*. Denver Publishing Company, 1986.

Murphy, Jan. *Outlaw Tales of Colorado*. Helena, Montana: Twodot—The Globe Pequot Press, 2006.

O'Connor, Richard. *Bat Masterson*. Garden City, New York: Doubleday & Company Inc., 1957.

Osgood, Ernest. *The Day of the Cattleman*. University of Chicago Press, 1929.

Patterson, Richard. *Historical Atlas of the Outlaw West*. Boulder: Johnson Books, 2002.

Perry, Elinor. *Colorado's Taylor Park Shangri-la*. Evergreen, Colorado: Shadow Canyon Graphics, 1989.

Perry, Elinor. *I Remember Tin Cup*. Gunnison, Colorado. B&B Printers, 1986.

Prassel, Frank Richard. *The Western Peace Officer*. Norman: University of Oklahoma Press, 1937.

Risse, Guenter; Numbers, Ronald; and Leavitt, Judith, Editors. *Medicine Without Doctors—Home Health Care in American History*. New York: Science History Publications USA, 1977.

Rockwell, Wilson. *Sunset Slope*. Ouray, Colorado: Western Reflections, Inc., 1999.

Rutler, Michael. *Upstairs Girls*. Helena, Montana: Farcountry Press, 2005.

Sammons, Judy Buffington. *Riding, Roping, and Roses—Colorado's Women Ranchers*. Lake City, Colorado: Western Reflections Publishing Company, 2006.

Sammons, Judy Buffington. *Tall Grass and Good Cattle—A Century of Ranching in the Gunnison Country*. Gunnison, Colorado: Dove Graphics, 2003.

Sarah Platt Decker Chapter D.A.R. *Pioneers of San Juan Country.* Colorado Springs: The Out West Printing & Stationery Company, 1942.

Schader, Conrad F. *Colorado's Alluring Tin Cup.* Regeo Alta Publications.

Shores, C.W., Ed. Rockwell, Wilson. *Memoirs of a Lawman.* Denver: Sage Books, 1962.

Stoddard, C.A. *Tales of the Old West Retold.* Montrose, Colorado: Lifetime Chronicle Press, 2007.

Tanner, Ogden. *The Ranchers.* Alexandria, Virginia: Time-Life Books, 1977.

Trachtman, Paul. *The Gunfighters.* Alexandria, Virginia: Time-Life Books, 1974.

Ubbelohde, Carl; Benson, Maxine; and Smith, Duane A. *A Colorado History.* Boulder: Pruett Publishing Company, 2006.

Vandenbusche, Duane and Smith, Duane A. *A Land Alone.* Boulder: Pruett Publishing Company, 1981.

Wallace, Betty. *Gunnison Country.* Denver: Sage Books, 1960.

Wallace, Betty. *History With the Hide Off.* Denver: Sage Books, 1965.

PERIODICALS/THESIS/MISCELLANEOUS

Bassett, Anne Willis. "Queen Anne of Brown's Park." *The Colorado Magazine,* April, 1952.

Bowles, Mildred Dolph. "Lewis and Mary Dolph." Unpublished Manuscript, April 4, 1998. Cedaredge Historical Society—Pioneer Town.

Borneman, Walter R. "Irwin: Silver Camp of the Ruby Mountains." Unpublished Masters thesis, May, 1975. Western State College Library.

Bryson, Kelly and Hoey, Janet, "The Truth Behind the 'Sons of Katy Elder.'" *Ptarmigan Quarterly, Inc.* Volume1, #3. Winter 1976.

Cornwall, Harry C. "The Gunnison Country—1879-1886." Unpublished Manuscript, 1928. Western State College Library.

Delta, Colorado City Cemetery—Information marker at the McCarty grave site.

Humphreys, Ray. "Trailing Colorado's Murderous Brothers." *Startling Detective Adventures*. December 1935.

"Memoirs of Judge John Gray 1841-1940." Compiled by Mary Olive Gray—1963.

Montrose County Historical Society. "The First County Jail" and "Sheriffs of Montrose County," by Betty Morris and Sue Nichol.

Pioneer Town at Cedaredge, Colorado. Printed information about the old Town Jail.

Rathmell, Ruth. "Of Record and Reminiscence—Ouray and Silverton."

The Saguache County Museum—printed information by Margaret B. Finnerty and Yvonne Halburian.

Stratton, Jeff. *An Early History of Western Law Enforcement—The Grand Junction, Colorado Police Department (1882-1930)*. Manuscript available at the Museum of Western Colorado Library, Grand Junction, Colorado.

Thompson, Thomas Gray. Master's Thesis: *Social and Cultural History of Lake City, Colorado— 1876-1900*. The University of Oklahoma Graduate College, Norman, Oklahoma, 1961.

Uncompahgre Frontier. Unpublished Manuscript by Wilson Rockwell. Circa 1950. Western State College Library.

NEWSPAPERS

Colorado West, "The Delta County Sheep War." 1973.

Gunnison Daily News-Democrat, June 18, 1882.

Gunnison Daily Review Press, May 7, 1883, August 2, 1884, and October 13, 1884.

Gunnison News Champion, May 16, 1917.

Gunnison Republican, July 25, 1901.

Gunnison Review, May 6, 1882.

Gunnison Tribune, June 7, and July 26, 1901.

Montrose Daily Press, March 13, 1929.

Ouray County Plaindealer and Herald, Ouray, Colorado, 1976.

Saguache Cresent. February 1930. Obituary of Samuel T. Ashley.

INTERVIEWS

Judy Buffington Sammons and Mitzie Gabriel, Cedaredge, Colorado, August 12, 2006.

Judy Buffington Sammons and Lawrence Phelps, Gunnison, Colorado, May, 1994.

About the Author

Judy Buffington Sammons lives in Gunnison, Colorado. She holds a Master of Arts Degree in Education and has recently retired from a thirty year teaching career in the field of Adult Education. Judy had written two other books: *Tall Grass and Good Cattle — A Century of Ranching in the Gunnison Country*, published by the Western State College Foundation and *Riding, Roping, and Roses — Colorado's Women Ranchers*, published by Western Reflections Publishing in 2006. Judy is a member of Western Writers of America.